Midrash Whispered by Stars

by

Bernd L. Bergmann

Dedication

There are moments in life when grace arrives not in thunder but in the quiet presence of one who listens deeply and walks beside you as a mirror of truth. To Theresa Marie Kelley - my wife, my spiritual companion, an Episcopal priest, whose soul moves with the rhythm of sacred mystery, thank you. Your guidance lit the path through the wilderness of this book, and your faith in the ineffable lent to my words their breath.

Preface

This book reaches beyond the boundaries of canon, threading its voice through the lesser-known gospels and sacred texts that whisper beneath tradition's surface. While the Gospel of Thomas is among the more prominent of these "Gnostic" writings, its inclusion here is merely the beginning. The narrative draws inspiration from a wide constellation of apocryphal sources among them the Gospel of Mary, the Gospel of Philip, the Gospel of Judas, the Gospel of the Egyptians, and the elusive Secret Gospel of Mark. And beyond these, potentially hundreds more, shrouded in obscurity, their fragments offering glimpses of an alternate sacred terrain.

Together, these texts form a chorus of forgotten echoes, each one a window into how mystery, divinity, and the human experience might once have been envisioned. This book listens to those echoes not as heresy but as possibility, crafting a story that honors the silence between scriptures as much as the words themselves.

Introduction: Midrash as Sacred Listening

Midrash Whispered By Stars is a work of interpretive devotion, a poetic Midrash that seeks not to explain Scripture, but to dwell within its mystery. In the Jewish tradition, Midrash is more than commentary; it is a sacred art form, a way of engaging the biblical text with imagination, reverence, and bold inquiry. It asks not only "What does this mean?" but "What might this mean for us now, in this moment, under these stars?"

This book stands in that lineage, though it is not bound by its academic conventions. It is Midrash in spirit, in posture, in yearning. Each chapter is a meditation—sometimes lyrical, sometimes narrative, sometimes theological, on passages that have stirred the soul across generations. These reflections do not seek to resolve the text, but to wrestle with it, to be transformed by it, and to let it speak anew.

The style is intentionally evocative. You may find echoes of rabbinic inquiry beside modern metaphor, ancient lament beside contemporary hope. The voices here are layered: Scripture, tradition, personal longing, and cosmic wonder. The stars in the title are not ornamental, they are symbolic of the vastness in which these questions live, and the quiet through which they are heard.

This Midrash is whispered, not shouted. It honors the silences of Scripture as much as its proclamations. It is written for those who believe that sacred texts are not relics, but living waters, flowing still, if we dare to listen.

You will not find rigid exegesis here. You will find awe. You will find grief. You will find the trembling joy of one who has walked long with the Word and still hears it calling. This book is offered in the spirit of spiritual stewardship. It is a gift of gratitude, for the texts that shaped us, the questions that haunt us, and the divine presence that meets us in both.

Contents

Chapter One - Inheritance of Clay

In a village balanced between forgotten time and unfolding eternity, where basalt stones kept the memory of every footfall and the air trembled with the quiet ache of waiting, a boy of five winters knelt beside a sun split patch of clay.

He had no name worth remembering at the time, only a presence too large for his small frame, as though the silence between stars had chosen a body, just to understand what it felt like to be five.

He moved as if listening to instructions older than language. His fingers, smudged with red earth, sculpted forms that seemed to emerge, rather than be made. Not birds in a child's crude image, but pigeons, city dwellers of heaven, with bodies shaped like questions, and necks iridescent like oil slicked prayer.

Each one bore the tension of arrested flight, wings bent mid beat, chests forward as if about to break some invisible curtain. They did not mimic life. They waited for it.

A boy from the village, feral with skepticism and knees scraped by lesser miracles, approached and scoffed. "Clay doesn't remember how to fly," he said. "It wasn't born." The child did not look up. His brow furrowed with the gravity of a candle listening for its own flame. He bent low and exhaled, not with breath, but with something denser, like memory speaking back into matter.

And the pigeons stirred.

It was not animation, it was recognition. As though the clay remembered its prehistory of wind and sky. Dust began to slough off like dead language. Wings twitched. Necks curved with sudden sentience. A low vibration, barely audible, sang through the courtyard, the frequency of stone softening.

Then, all at once, they rose.

Not with flapping or struggle, but with inevitability. Like ideas once trapped in logic suddenly liberated by meaning. The pigeons lifted in spirals, carving impossible geometry in the air, fractal arcs of gray and violet, looping like benedictions above the rooftops.

The villagers emerged, tools half lowered, mouths half formed into disbelief. One woman bowed low, uttering words in a dialect older than the scrolls of Moses. An elder dropped his walking stick and whispered a psalm he hadn't dared recite since the war. The boy watched, his face unreadable, not with secrecy, but with the luminous simplicity of fire before it knew it gave off light.

That evening, under lamps burning olive oil and wonder, his mother brushed flecks of clay from his tunic. "They will ask who you are," she said softly. The child did not smile. "They already know," he said. "They just haven't remembered yet."

And in that village where pigeons would sometimes land in circles too perfect for chance, cooing as if repeating some buried invocation. The tale was retold by those who had seen and those who had only almost believed.

None spoke the boy's name.

But later, when stones rolled and tombs could not hold what had always been moving toward the sky, a few whispered, "We should have known. Even the pigeons told us."

Chapter Two - The Well of the Unspoken Name

There was a well on the outskirts of the village, though some argued it was the village that had grown outward to escape it. Its stones were older than empire, mortared with ash and hearsay, veined by roots that remembered Eden even if no tongue dared say so. Children called it cursed. Elders called it sacred. No one drank from it.

They had forgotten why.

The slab covering its mouth was wide and smooth, worn down by wind, prayer, and silence in equal measure. Upon it, moss clung like hesitant theology, and lines once etched with holy names now traced only the erosion of belief. It had not been opened since before the last famine, perhaps longer. The elders would say, with voices like cracked parchment, that something in the water had once stolen a man's memory. But others, quiet ones, strange ones, said the water had only revealed what he had labored his whole life to forget.

The boy approached at midmorning, alone, though the air around him thickened as if in accompaniment. He was of slight frame, with feet barely dusted and garments that gathered light like second skin. But it was his stillness that the villagers would later speak of. Not the slowness of a child at play, but the density of something vast choosing not to overwhelm.

He was six then, not in numbers marked on stone, but in the sixth unfolding of winter since first breath had lodged itself inside him, uneasy with the narrowness of his frame. His hands were small but carried the hesitancy of a creator remembering the fragile holiness of beginnings.

He did not knock at the stone. He listened.

He placed his palm flat on its face and leaned in, not in scrutiny, but in reunion. The hush around him grew tense, as though the earth itself dared not interrupt. Then, without spectacle, he exhaled, not wind, but something denser, a remembrance, pressed into vibration. It entered the stone like an old psalm sung backwards.

The air shifted.

A low tremor began beneath their feet, not violent, but mournful, like a shofar blown by the bones of those who had never been buried properly. Cracks spread across the slab, not as fractures, but as inscriptions reappearing. The moss pulled back. Dust lifted. And the stone slid aside with the gravity of a veil choosing to rend itself. Darkness yawned beneath.

A rope descended, not unwound from spindle or hook, but spun midair from fibers unseen. It dangled, slack and waiting, then tugged itself downward into the waiting throat of the world.

When it rose again, the bucket bore water clear as the first dew of creation, undisturbed by time, trembling only slightly, as though unsure if it should make itself known.

They came.

At first, only one or two, an old widow who had not spoken her husband's name aloud since the locusts came, and a mute boy who dreamed of songs without knowing language. They dipped their fingers cautiously, then gasped-not from chill, but from recognition.

The woman wept and whispered, "It tastes like his laughter in our wedding tent."

The boy hummed a single sustained note no one had ever taught him.

Birds overhead adjusted their flight.

More came.

A blind man laughed at the color he remembered.

A carpenter's apprentice confessed a lie he had not known he'd buried.

One by one, they drank and remembered - not events, but being. Not images, but the meaning beneath them. Words long exiled from tongue found sanctuary in throat. Names spoken only in wombs were named aloud, as if they had been waiting for this water to be born again. And the boy watched. Not in triumph. Not in detachment. But in quiet ache. As though he carried the burden of unveiling too much to a world too fragile to hold it.

A teacher among them approached and, kneeling not to the child, but to the moment, asked, "What do we call this?" The child did not answer immediately. His gaze fell back into the well, into the depths where time had no purchase. Then, soft but steady, he said, "It once knew its name. I only spoke it again."

"And you? What are you?" the teacher asked.

The boy's eyes lifted, dark and unblinking, like stars remembering how to burn. "I am what cannot be forgotten."

That evening, the village held no feast, no formal rite. Instead, they gathered by the well and each, in turn, whispered a name they feared the world had lost. Not always human names, sometimes a field's old name before conquest, or the word their mother used for joy that had no translation. They did not explain. They did not debate meaning. They simply released the names into the air.

And the stars leaned in.

The water remained; clear and waiting. The bucket no longer needed rope, it rose when called. Animals drank from it and watched the horizon for signs. Travelers began arriving, led by dreams they couldn't explain, claiming they had heard songs in languages without vowels.

As for the boy, he did not stay. He was found the next day near a stream, tracing circles in the mud and asking a frog if it remembered leaping the first time it knew it could.

His mother arrived quietly, brushing the clay from his fingers. She asked no questions, only pressed her forehead to his and whispered a word that made the olive trees shiver. And though no one spoke his name aloud, they began referring to him in whispers and glances, in pauses before lighting lamps, in the breath held after final prayers. They didn't know what to call him.

But deep down, beneath the noise and the hunger and the keeping of ledgers, they began to remember why they had once needed a name at all.

Chapter Three - Beneath the Rib of Eden

He was seven, though years clung to him like smoke, seen more by their fragrance than their weight. The sun had begun its slow descent into barley colored dusk, and dust slept in the creases of every robe and eyelid. That day, the wind tasted of distant citrus, as if angels somewhere had peeled oranges while weeping.

The boy stood barefoot in the valley beyond the carpenter's shed, where the wild sheep no longer grazed and stones wept quietly into themselves. The earth here was cracked, not broken, but aching, as if something once buried had begun to stir beneath it again. Beneath his feet, the ground crunched with seed husks and forgotten pilgrim tears.

He had brought with him no tools, no scrolls. Only a single almond in his pocket and the silence that always seemed to follow him, as though the world itself was trying to remember how to breathe around him.

The elders had spoken of this place with muttered references, calling it the Elam Grove, though no Elam had lived for generations. They said the trees here had been cursed to bear no fruit after a priest buried his shame beneath them. Others said the trees had never borne fruit because the soil still mourned something it could not name.

But the boy, still more question than boy, walked among the trunks like he was tracing veins on the wrist of creation.

He paused by the oldest tree. Its bark was blackened, not from fire, but from time itself trying to erase its memory. Deep grooves carved it like forgotten text, each notch the echo of an exile, each knot a sealed promise. He laid his palm on its trunk, as he had the stone that veiled the well. But this time, he didn't listen. He remembered.

And the tree responded.

Its roots trembled, not with hunger, but recognition. Dust lifted from its bark in soft spirals, and a sound came, not rustling, not cracking, but groaning. The kind the earth made when it remembered its first agony, being split to birth a rib. From beneath the gnarled roots, the soil began to loosen. Not from digging or decay, but from invitation. A cavity yawned open beneath the tree, and young boy stepped into it, not with hesitation, but like one returning to the womb of an old hymn.

What he found beneath was not a cave, nor a tomb, but something older, a chamber carved not by human hands, but by longing. Its walls were latticed with roots that pulsed faintly, like veins still dreaming of Eden. And at its center lay a rib, not human, not animal, but something stranger.

Long as a shepherd's crook, translucent as fresh honeycomb, it glowed faintly in the dim. Around it, the air tasted of bronze and crushed myrrh. He knelt, not to worship, but to remember, because that was what this relic demanded, not belief, but memory. He reached out, and as his fingers touched the rib, images, no, impressions coursed through him, a garden where names had weight and walked alongside their bearers, a silence that hummed with every word not yet spoken, the moment when flesh first knew it was not alone.

Then came the ache.

Not pain, but the ache of having once been whole and remembering it. He wept, not in sorrow, but with reverence. Because he now knew, this rib had not been taken from Adam. It had been given; a fragment of divine loneliness made matter, tucked beneath the orchard's soil by the One who could no longer walk in the cool of the day without shattering the sky with grief.

This was not the rib of Eve's making.

This was the rib God buried when Eden was sealed, to keep one memory untouched by exile.

And he had found it.

Aboveground, the almond trees bloomed all at once. Every branch exhaled white fire, and petals fell like forgotten blessings.

Villagers came running, led not by miracles but by instincts older than fear.

They found him seated beneath the oldest tree, soil streaking his cheeks like war paint made of resurrection. In his lap, the rib shone dimly, pulsing in time with the setting sun.

A woman knelt, a midwife who had once seen a child born with no cry. She reached out to touch the rib, but the boy whispered, "Not yet. It remembers too much." She bowed, understanding nothing and everything.

A scribe from Sepphoris arrived, breathless and trembling. He had been transcribing lost psalms when a voice like oil on stone told him, "Go. Listen beneath the almond trees."

He asked the boy, "Is it... is it the lost bone of the First Covenant?"

The boy smiled faintly, though his eyes remained somber, "It is what was set aside when we were still made of trust."

That night, no one slept. The villagers did not feast, nor pray aloud. They simply walked among the trees, placing their hands on trunks and whispering things they had never told even themselves.

One man confessed to a stone that he had once hidden bread from his starving brother.

A child hummed a melody she claimed the stars had given her in a dream.

And the trees listened.

By morning, the rib was gone, not stolen, not buried again, but absorbed. The oldest tree now had a single branch that glowed faintly, as if caught perpetually in moonrise. And the boy? He was found by the river again, this time weaving reeds into a crown and setting it adrift. When asked what he was doing, he answered, "Sending a reminder forward in time. Someone will need it."

Chapter Four - The Dust at His Heels

At eight winters, the boy called Yeshua by some and Netzer, the Shoot, a name derived from ancient scrolls, by others, wore silence like a garment. Not the silence of shyness, but the ancient stillness of unstruck flint. He belonged to no place but the edge of things: the hem of his mother's cloak, the threshold of his father's doorframe, the shimmer where the desert kissed the olive groves east of the ridge called Har HaBayit.

It was the season when figs began to blush. Dust hung in the air not as nuisance, but as presence, fine, warm, and scented with sheep, sweat, and cedar. The elders of the village, leaning like weathered columns against limestone walls, spoke often of Rome with spit in their beards and prophecy in their voices. But the boy listened instead to the gaps between their words, where truth hides like a coin in the dust.

He often wandered to the well before first light. There, old Miryam, the widow who claimed her dreams came wrapped in fire once said to him, "When the sky was newborn, it whispered its promise to the earth, 'I shall reflect you, if you can bear to be seen.'" He never forgot those words. He did not know then that he, too, had once made a promise. One uttered before bones, before breath, before Bethlehem.

17

Each morning, he spoke softly to the stones by the roadside as if they were awaiting instruction, "You will remember me when sandals press prophecy into your backs." And though the stones did not answer, the wind moved differently after he passed, like an old rabbi lifting his head mid-prayer.

In the marketplace, he touched no money, yet vendors gave him dates split open to reveal golden flesh. One potter claimed the boy's gaze left fingerprints on the clay before it hardened in the sun. "There is something in his eyes," she told her husband, "like a tomorrow that remembers."

Once, a Roman tribune riding through Nazareth with dust-caked arrogance locked eyes with the child. The soldier's stallion reared unprovoked, and the man cursed, only to find the boy unmoved. Later, the tribune would speak of it in hushed Latin, "He looked at me not as one threatened, but as one who mourned my ruin before I arrived at it."

The boy's earthly father, a builder who measured twice and spoke little, watched him with the wary awe of one entrusted with fire wrapped in lambswool. "You are too still for one so small," he said once, "like a hill that knows it will be climbed." To which the boy replied, "Then let me be good earth under aching feet."

He learned letters not from scribes, but from shadows cast by oil lamps on cave walls. He traced them backward, right to left like the path home after exile. Each letter he memorized he whispered into olive branches and fig leaves, as though preparing them to receive voices centuries yet unborn.

He asked once why the scrolls were hidden in the Ark. The rabbi answered, "Because some truths must be wrapped in holiness lest they break the world." The boy nodded slowly. "And some truths," he murmured, "must be broken to feed it."

As harvest neared, a man in rags came limping through the village. No one touched him, he was marked by the grey tremble of skin unclean. The boy approached, knelt, and spoke not healing, but memory, "Before the hills were set in place, you laughed in the presence of the Voice." The man wept, not from cure, but from being remembered. When he left, his limp remained, but so did his smile.

On the evening of his eighth birthday, a storm rolled across the horizon but never reached the village. He stood on the threshold of the house, eyes toward thunder, and said quietly, "The sky is clearing its throat."

His mother, young and ancient all at once, placed her hand on his shoulder and whispered, "What are you becoming?" And he, barely breathing, replied, "A reply to a promise."

That night he dreamed of a ladder not built of wood but of breaths, each rung a whisper kept. Angels neither climbed nor descended it; they wept beside it, for they knew what promises cost when they wear flesh.

At dawn he awoke to the smell of cumin and soaked lentils, the clay walls of the house exhaling their warmth like a second skin. Outside, roosters announced nothing new, yet he stepped into the morning as though it was creation's first unveiling. A neighbor's goat bleated in complaint, tied too tightly to a fig trunk. The boy paused and loosened the cord. Freedom, even for beasts, was a kind of prophecy.

That day his father took him to the quarry beyond the acacia line. The rocks, shattered from ages of chisel and praise, bore striations like the scrolls of Sinai. "Choose one." said the father. "A cornerstone is not found. It is chosen." The boy placed his hand upon a fragment veined with white. "This one trembles when touched," he said. "as if remembering what it was."

His father nodded slowly but said nothing. Some truths, he knew, should only be answered by silence.

As they walked home, the boy recited sayings he had collected, not written ones, but those carried on breath and ash:

"The wind listens to the faithful."

"Memory is the shape water leaves when it flees."

"The promise does not age, only the one who waits for it."

That evening, a traveling weaver came with tales from the salt rimmed shores of the western sea. His stories curved like mosaics, full of Leviathans and kingdoms drowned in pride. The boy listened long, eyes tracing the fray at the edge of the man's cloak. When asked what he thought of the tales, he said softly, "Even beasts obey borders drawn by mercy."

The village elders took note of him more often now.

One asked, "Child, do you believe you are meant for something?" He looked not at the elder, but at the empty bowl beside him. "Everything meant something before we named it," he answered.

That next morning, the light came down thick as fig resin, gilding the hills and adobe walls in gold not found in coin. It was the hour before roosters dared speak. Bread rose slowly in a clay oven's belly, giving off its scent like an offering. Ash from sandalwood fires still clung to the corners of the hearth like breath unwilling to leave. The child, still unnamed by the world yet named before the world was, rose without summons. He moved with the hush of prayer, not silence from absence, but silence from fullness. When he stepped barefoot onto the threshold, he paused. Every crossing felt eternal. He stared out toward the horizon with the look of someone waiting, not for footsteps, but for the hour itself to remember.

His mother passed behind him, brushing flour from her hands, and laid her fingers briefly atop his curls. A wordless gesture that said, "You were given to me, but not kept for me." She did not ask where he would go. A child born beneath hallelujahs must be followed, not led.

His father, broad across the back like the yoke of the land, lifted a length of cedar. "The lintel must be set before the sun catches it," he said. The child nodded, "A doorway bears not only wood, but the memory of welcome. Let it be carved by hands that tremble with reverence."

They set off toward the grove. The fields were waking, young barley glistened with dew, and bees murmured mid blessing. Alongside the road, almond trees whispered in first bloom. He trailed his fingers across their bark and whispered greetings, not to the trees, but to what the trees remembered, the garden, the exile, the promise.

Along the way they passed a man bent low beneath a bundle of wood, back shaped by burdens not meant for one man. The child stepped forward unasked and lifted the load with a grace that defied flesh. The man stared. "Why help me?" he rasped. The boy replied, "Because the beginning of kindness is remembering we were never strangers."

Together they walked until the man's path turned. He looked back once and said, "The earth forgets most footsteps. Yours it will cradle like a prayer."

Later, beneath the cedar grove's hush, the father began measuring the timber. The child knelt near a scrap of cast-off wood, tracing its grain with a fingertip. "Wood bears memory," he murmured. "It weeps in its rings."

"What do you see?" his father asked.

"A door." the child answered, "And behind it, all we have longed for."

"You speak like the prophets," his father said.

"No," the boy said gently, "I speak like one who listened when they did."

They lingered until the sun slanted bronze through the trees and the shadows thickened like ink across a scroll. On the road home, they came upon two boys wrestling in dust, fury blind on their faces. Neither remembered the quarrel's origin. The child stepped between them, placed one hand on each brow, and whispered, "The wound you carry was never yours."

The boys froze, their breaths stilled before they parted. The older asked, "What tribe do you belong to?" "I belong to the promise," the boy said. "And the One who keeps it."

That night, oil lamps flickered inside homes pressed close together like verses in a psalm. The boy sat beneath the new lintel they had raised, his eyes tracing stars as they peeled away from the dark. Each was a covenant still burning.

An elder, a once scribe whose fingers now shook from age, sat beside him. "You," the old man said, eyes clouded, "do you know the Shema?" The boy's voice rose like a wind made whole, "Shema Yisrael, Adonai Eloheinu, Adonai Echad." The elder wept quietly. "I used to write those words in ink." he whispered, "They declare the One who binds us. You speak them in flame." The boy replied, "The words never left the fire. We simply forgot how to burn."

That night, the boy dreamed again. Not the hazy drift of sleep, but the ancient remembering that happens in eternity's marrow. He stood beside a river with no source and no mouth. Upon its current floated syllables, Aleph, Tav, secret tetragrams that glowed like molten covenants.

From within the river came a voice, "Do you remember the vow?"

Another voice, his own, or perhaps the One that breathed him into dust answered, "He remembers, so we endure."

When he awoke the hearth coals had arranged themselves into the shape of a vine twisting skyward.

That week, a caravan passed through Nazareth from Damascus, traders with spices wrapped in palm leaf bundles and scrolls sealed in wax. Among them was a scholar wrapped in dusk-colored robes, a man who had stared at Torah until his eyelashes turned pale. He had heard of the boy, the one who spoke to wind and wept beside stone. He found him near the village well, whispering to a pigeon whose wing hung limp like torn cloth.

The scholar watched. He expected magic. He witnessed something else.

"Boy," he said at last, "what use is speech to birds?"

The child did not look up, "Words remind wings what they were made for."

Intrigued, the man crouched closer, "And you, what were you made for?"

The child raised his eyes then, eyes that held the glint of Sinai's fire and the sadness of Eden's gate and said, "To become the pause between the Name and its echo."

The scholar shuddered. He had traced every letter of Isaiah, wrestled the syntax of Ezekiel. But he had never heard theology uttered like breath.

When the caravan departed, he left behind a scroll blank but for one word, Zakhar, remember, sealed in wax and silence. He handed it to the boy's father and said, "For when he chooses to write what we cannot bear to forget."

Later that week, the fever came for a child six winters old, with curls like coiled olive leaves. She died before sunrise. No prayer was fast enough. No sage wise enough. The wailing cleaved the morning. The boy stood outside the house, unmoving. He did not knock. He placed his palm upon the threshold and whispered, "She is not lost. Only held somewhere words can't follow."

Then he walked away.

That night, her mother, torn by grief, dreamed of a garden where the fig trees hummed with dew, and her daughter laughed among lilies. When she awoke, her hands smelled faintly of warm bread and cumin.

A week later, beneath the scaffold of the lintel they had set, the father asked, "When shall I teach you to cut stone?"

The child stared at his hands, steady, expectant, born both before and after trembling.

"When stone remembers I've always known how," he said.

The father nodded once, and so the chiseling began, not with muscle, but with memory.

The first stone the boy shaped bore a scar across its belly, a hairline crack running through it.

"Should we discard it?" his father asked.

The boy placed his fingers gently across the flaw.

"No," he said, "This one remembers being broken. It will hold our weight."

By the end of that moon, he stopped asking questions, not because the world grew dull, but because creation had begun answering in its own liturgy: oil breathing in lamplight, reeds whispering along the Jordan, wind changing its gait to match a boy's footsteps.

And those who watched him said strange things,

"He walks like someone who's already come back."

"He speaks to sorrow like it owes him worship."

"There's dust at his heels that glows when the stars rise."

But he himself never claimed to be the Promise. He was only the echo of its making.

The remembering that kept it alive.

The prophecy the silence could no longer contain.

Chapter Five - The Cave of the Listening Flame

The boy was nine, and the world had begun to whisper in a different tongue.

It was not the Aramaic of his mother's lullabies, nor the Hebrew of the scrolls he traced with reverent fingers. It was older than syllables, older than breath. It came in the hush between hammer strikes in the carpenter's shed, in the wind that sifted through olive branches like a hand through hair, in the silence that followed the bleating of a lamb just before the blade.

He had begun to hear it at dusk, when the sun bled itself dry across the hills and the stones turned the color of old wounds. It was not a voice, not exactly. It was a pull, a gravity of the soul, drawing him beyond the perimeter of the known.

And so, he walked.

He walked past the threshing floor where men bent like question marks over their labor, their hands shaped by the silence between commandments. He walked past the well where women drew water with the same rhythm their mothers had taught them; their laughter echoing like psalms with missing verses.

He walked until the village was a memory behind him, and the earth rose into hills that had not forgotten the footsteps of prophets.

The sand here was not soft. It bit at his ankles, clung to his tunic, insinuated itself into the creases of his skin like a second baptism. The sun, though descending, still ruled the sky with tyrannical heat, and each step was a negotiation between will and weariness.

But he did not stop.

There was something ahead, he did not know what, only that it had been waiting for him since before he was born. He found the cave just as the last light died.

It was not marked by sign or shrine. No altar stood at its mouth, no inscription warned or welcomed. It was simply there, as if the earth had exhaled and left behind a hollow in its breath. The entrance yawned like a question too sacred to be asked aloud.

He stepped inside.

The air changed. It was cooler, yes, but also denser, thick with the scent of ash and something older than fire. The walls were roughhewn, veined with mineral seams that shimmered faintly in the dark like veins of forgotten light. He moved deeper, his fingers brushing the stone, reading it like scripture.

And then he saw it.

At the center of the cave, there was a flame. It did not flicker. It did not consume. It burned with a stillness that defied wind and time. It was not fed by oil or wick. It simply was. A presence, not a phenomenon. It cast no shadows, and yet it illuminated everything.

He sat before it.

He did not speak. He did not pray. He simply listened.

And in that listening, the world began to unravel.

He heard the weeping of exiled angels, the laughter of stars being born, the groaning of the earth as it bore the weight of unspoken names. He heard the breath of the Father, not as thunder or command, but as a silence so vast it made language tremble.

A voice, not from the flame, but from within the silence, spoke,

"You are not here to learn. You are here to remember."

He did not ask who spoke. He knew. It was the voice that had called him into being, the voice that had sung the cosmos into its spiraling dance, the voice that had once said, "Let there be!" and now whispered, "Let there be you."

Another voice joined it, softer, rounder, like water over stone, "The Anthropos is not a man. It is the memory of what man was meant to be."

He turned, and there she was.

A woman, or the memory of one. Veiled in shadow, robed in light. Her eyes held galaxies, and her hands bore the dust of creation. She did not speak with her mouth, but with her presence. She was Sophia, or Mary, or the Shekhinah. She was the feminine breath of God, the echo of wisdom before the world began.

She knelt beside him.

"You will be called many things:" she said, "Rabbi. Rebel. Redeemer. But before all that, you are the Listener."

He looked into the flame.

"What is it?" he asked.

"It is flame before judgment," she said. "Light before it chooses to consume."

He reached out. The flame did not scorch. It welcomed.

And in that moment, he remembered.

He remembered the silence before the first word. He remembered the ache of divine separation, the longing of God to be known in flesh. He remembered the covenant not written in stone, but in breath.

He remembered himself.

That night, sleep came slowly, like a guest who enters without knocking.

He lay beneath the open sky, the roof of the house warm with the breath of the day. The stars above him were not distant, they were near, like eyes that had forgotten how to close. He watched them until the watching became dreaming.

And in that dream, he stood again at the mouth of the cave.

But this time, the cave was not carved into stone. It was carved into the sky.

The stars had gathered into an arch, and the flame burned at the center of the heavens.

It was not fire now, but a scroll, sealed, unreadable, alive. It pulsed with the rhythm of breath, as if waiting to be spoken.

He reached for it, but his hands were small again, smaller than they had ever been.

Infant hands. Swaddled in light.

A voice, neither male nor female, neither near nor far, whispered, "You will speak what cannot be written. You will carry what cannot be taught."

The scroll unraveled, but instead of words, it revealed a face.

His own.

But older. Weathered. Wounded. Radiant.

The stars wept.

And he woke.

The sky was still dark, but the first thread of dawn had begun to stitch itself across the horizon. He sat up slowly, the dream still clinging to his skin like dew. He did not speak of it.

He never did.

Chapter Six - The Oracular Youth

Upon the tenth revolution of seasons since his first breath, the Child moved among the elders as a cipher cloaked in flesh, the embodiment of primordial utterance veiled in the subtle weakness of bone. To those whose eyes did not see, he was only boy, yet to those who listened beneath the visible, he stood as revelation unspoken.

He walked not upon the earth, but through it, his passage leaving no mark, yet carving memory into the grain of dust. The desert, in its infinite vocabulary, curled around his ankles and declared him known. The wind, having wandered unmastered since the forging of the skies, paused to listen, then departed burdened by comprehension.

One said, "He speaks, yet no mouth moves. He teaches, yet no parchment bears his hand."

Another replied, "He is not the scholar, he is the question itself."

The elders, possessors of doctrines ossified through centuries, inquired with suspicion, "By what tutelage do you offer such truths?" His response resounded not in sound but in silence whose depth unsettled the stars. "Knowledge," he said, "is the echo of intimacy, not instruction. It is the remembrance of that which never began."

He took nothing with him but attention, and wherever he cast his gaze, the elements rearranged themselves as if reminded of their source. Fig trees blossomed in errorless obedience. Hills, once silent, sang the vowels of creation. His fingers traced the soil, and it opened, yielding its wisdom not through words but through sensation. It was said by one who watched in trembling awe, "He caressed the land as if consoling memory itself, and memory wept."

A philosopher, veined with years and pride, approached him, asking, "What is existence without essence?" The Child replied, "It is shadow searching for light it once was."

He did not speak of divinity, for divinity was imprisoned by language. He did not preach salvation, for salvation was understood by his breath alone. He stood, and reality adjusted to accommodate the weight of his silence.

In the deep country where stars hum louder and thought bleeds into sky, he was found alone, conversing with the void. And from that void came a voice, not alien but familiar, saying, "Before the division of fire and water, you were the pulse." He nodded, not in agreement but in affirmation of what had never been forgotten.

That night, as the moon unveiled itself like revelation made visible, he declared to no one and to all, "Let every atom know it dreams of return." And the wind, astonished by coherence, danced.

A woman mourning her son approached, her sorrow vast as night. She asked, "Can grief be undone?" He placed a hand upon the earth and said, "Grief is not wound, but doorway." She understood, and for the first time in decades, breathed.

A poet inscribed upon limestone, "He wears eternity like skin, and his voice is the language of origin."

The sand, clinging to his feet, did not fall away. It remained, as if consecrated. Each grain bore witness to mysteries too vast for articulation. Those who dared touch that sand afterward claimed visions, and one wrote, "I tasted the ground and found it sweet."

He stood upon a ridge where ancient flames once spoke to dreamers and uttered a declaration so immense the stones beneath cracked not in violence, but in joy, "I am not future; I am not past. I am the breath between remembrance and longing."

They did not understand, and yet they followed.

In that age, he was called many things:

Son of the Aeon

Voice of the Unbegotten

Flame of Knowing

Child of Silence.

But never was his true name spoken, for his name was not made of letters, but of the infinite spaces between them.

Then came the day when the heavens bowed, not with storm but with silence so thick the birds forgot to fly. The Youth stood upon the edge of the valley where light and shadow braided their eternal discourse, and the air trembled with longing.

There, amid rocks unshaped by man and winds unclaimed by map, he spoke words not composed but remembered. His voice, still slight as a reed in rain, unfurled a truth that made the stars clutch their breath, "What is shall not perish, for it was never made. And what was made shall fade, for it dreamed itself real."

Those nearby did not respond. They fell inward, their minds unfastened, their hearts weeping for a truth they could not bear.

An old shepherd, blind since boyhood, approached on trembling feet. The Youth placed a hand over his eyes and said, "Sight is not a gift of flesh, but of remembrance. Look not with gaze, but with origin." The man opened his lids and saw. Not color, not form, but truth itself walking as a boy beside him.

One scribe, devoted to ink and order, attempted to write what he witnessed. His hands betrayed him. His parchment curled. His letters scattered. Later, in despair and awe, he declared, "I tried to write eternity. It swallowed the pen."

The Youth entered the river that ran older than memory. As his feet touched water it ceased its flow, startled by recognition. He whispered to the current, "You have wandered long enough. Return not to source but become it." And the water, shimmering with a forgotten clarity, resumed, not flowing, but becoming.

He stood beneath an ancient fig tree, its limbs bent low with stories. It asked, "Will men ever know?" He replied, "Men will ask forever. Knowing is the stillness between the questions."

That night, fireflies traced circles around him, forming symbols never known. The sky opened not in storm, but in invitation. And he spoke one final utterance, soft as breath, brutal as birth, "The veil is no longer torn. It was never there."

These words spread without voice. They entered the bones of men and the rings of trees. They were etched into mountain stone without hand, carried by the wind like forgotten hymns. Across generations they traveled, not as knowledge, but as ache.

A seer in a distant land awoke, weeping, crying out, "I have heard the breath before speech."

And a child, newly born, gazed upward and did not cry, for it remembered.

The Youth walked on. No footprints remained. But the earth, ever changed, still sings his passage. When the mountains no longer held their breath and the stars abandoned their distance, the Child ascended the highest rise in the desert, where silence wore a crown and time knelt in awe. The air thickened with memory, every particle burdened with what had been and what must never be spoken. Night stretched its wings, not to cover but to consecrate. He stood alone, yet all creation leaned forward. Ravens paused in flight; their wings carved from stillness. The sand arranged itself into sacred geometry, patterns older than alphabet and untouched by calculation. The wind carried the scent of beginnings, of clay before command, of light before color.

He raised his hands and the sky shivered. No thunder came, only the groan of eternity bending to listen. He spoke, "Matter is the echo of longing." Spirit is the remembrance of origin. Between them lies the ache called living." The sky wept golden, not rain but memory, the release of wisdom bound too long in solitude.

The Youth touched the earth with both hands and breathed a word never written, a word that turned blood into light and shadow into language. Those nearby felt themselves dismantled, not destroyed but revealed. An infant in a village miles away awakened with eyes wide, speaking truths in a tongue no one knew but everyone understood.

An elder, mute since war, began to chant.

A tree bloomed in winter.

Time fractured for a moment, revealing the breath behind all becoming.

Then the Youth turned to the east and said, "Do not seek my face, for you shall find only your own. I am not path; I am the question that makes paths necessary."

The moon dimmed in reverence.

Rivers stopped pretending to flow.

Stars blinked as if unsure they belonged in such a tapestry. He walked forward, but no ground received him. He stepped into memory itself. He entered the hush between thought and word. His departure was not seen but felt, like gravity lifting its hand from the soul.

Later, when the scribes gathered, their pages empty but hearts full. One said, "We must write what we cannot write."

Another answered, "We must remember what none of us saw."

And a third, ancient and trembling, whispered, "Let us become the silence he left behind."

The sands never forgot. The wind still carries his breath. Every truth since has been a ripple from that moment when mystery wore a child's form and the world wept because it finally recognized its own reflection.

In a glade where the silence grew tall like trees, a doe approached, its eyes wide with a memory it did not earn. The animal did not flinch, it remained still, and the air around it folded like fabric warmed by breath. The Youth did not touch it, and yet it knew him.

Clouds gathered above with no threat, only presence, their softness bending like patience across the sky. They did not weep, they observed, drifting as if pushed by some forgotten kindness.

At the bend of a river, old fishermen lowered their nets and sat upon stones polished smooth by years. One whispered to the other, not in awe, but in recognition, "That is not the boy, that is what the boy becomes when silence pays attention."

The Youth touched a leaf fallen from no branch, and it lifted itself once again, shimmering not from light but from memory too pure to stay hidden. Trees nearby shivered, not from wind but from knowing. Their roots dug deeper, clinging to stories beneath the soil.

Far off, a woman writing letters to her lost child paused, then began again. Her pen did not tremble, but her fingers curled as if cradling something long buried. The ink no longer recorded sorrow, it measured arrival.

In a field where wheat leaned into dusk, the wind lifted grains and suspended them mid-air, holding a shape that looked like breath holding a thought. Children watched, their laughter softened, their eyes widened, their mouths forgot speech.

He passed through a canyon, its walls smooth as glass, yet etched with names no human knew. The names pulsed faintly, not with light, but with warmth. The traveler touched one and felt his own birth again, but without pain.

The Youth knelt by a spring where water ran upward, then downward, without losing itself. He did not drink, but the ripples pressed outward, as if his presence stirred time and made it fluid.

A dog with no collar sat beside him, and when he stood, it did not follow. It remained still, tail tucked beneath its body, eyes closed. Behind it, a flock of birds turned mid-flight, forming a spiral above the ridge. Their wings caught no air, only intention.

The dusk arrived like a whisper in motion, folding itself over the fields with the grace of regret. He did not speak to it, but the light dimmed slowly, not in sadness, but in agreement.

A stone trembled where he stepped, not broken, only awake. Beneath it, ants paused mid-harvest, circled once, then resumed, their path now changed, their course realigned.

He passed a gardener who had once forgotten the names of her plants. Now each bloom turned slightly toward him, petals unfolding before dawn, dew forming early, as if time had been persuaded.

Mountains watched. They did not lower themselves, but leaned in ever so slightly, their peaks humming with age and memory.

A climber resting near the summit felt a rush of calm, then wrote nothing in his journal, only staring and breathing.

A child built a tower of feathers beside the lake, each one balanced without aid. When the youth passed, a wind stirred but did not break the tower. Instead, it lifted one feather and set it in motion. The child nodded, not with joy, but with understanding.

Gravel beneath his feet warmed gently, as if greeting rather than resisting. The path did not stretch ahead it folded behind him, shrinking as if to preserve its own story.

Across valleys, across forgotten edges of maps, his movement registered not in coordinates, but in adjustments. Time moved slower, rivers bent wider, birds slept later. All without instruction, all without cause.

A sculptor chipping away at marble paused, his chisel floating above the stone. He closed his eyes and saw not shape, but breath forming structure.

The sculpture remained incomplete, yet perfect.

He stood once more beneath a sky swirling with clouds, and though the moon had not risen, its light traced his outline. Not shadow, not glow, but something in between. Stars waited, refusing to blink. A girl drawing circles in the dust looked up as he passed. Her circles stretched and changed, forming symbols not learned but recognized. She did not look away, and her circles did not stop.

Rain fell, not from storm, but from memory. Each drop carried weight, scent, and origin. Nothing was drowned, only renewed. Puddles did not reflect sky, they reflected attention.

A woman weaving cloth found that her threads adjusted, became finer, stronger. Her patterns curved into meanings, though she had not chosen them. She set her loom aside, walked toward the open field, and stood still.

The Youth continued. No voice called after him, no guide beckoned. Yet stones tilted, branches leaned, even wind curved. He did not ask for directions, but direction formed around him.

A canyon split, not with violence, but with birth. Its walls sang, not music, but texture. Those who entered found echoes of their own footsteps returned before they had walked.

He walked into fog and the fog parted, not because he commanded it, but because it remembered him.

The mist carried fragments of stories not yet spoken.

Voices formed, not in air, but in awareness.

The night grew quiet, not empty, just ready. Beneath it, seeds turned in the soil, roots stretched, and even the stars burned steadier.

He walked until walking became still.

And in the stillness, the world exhaled.

Chapter Seven - The Voices That Do Not Cry Out

The morning began with wind, not loud but old, brushing over the river stone with breath that remembered Eden. Beneath the cedars near the low ridge, the boy, who was called Yeshu'a in the tongue of elders, stood bare footed, watching how the light refused to rush. It did not conquer the shadows. It sat beside them, as if they were kin.

He was eleven years carried from the womb, but there were no measures in him. Time had not yet taught him to divide things. Instead, he felt the world as a pulse without border. Each leaf trembled, not with fear but with knowing. Each breeze did not blow past him, it passed through him, as if the wilderness had decided he belonged.

He stepped further from the low encampment where stones had been gathered for last night's fire. That fire had been brief, not for warmth but for story. And even then, no one had spoken. Only the flame told the tale, lifting sparks toward a sky that always listened but never interrupted.

The boy walked softly. He knew the ground beneath him remembered floods. He knew the trees above had once bent beneath snowfall so heavy it reshaped silence. And he knew something else; the silence today was not mute. It was thinking. When he reached the bend in the river, he did not kneel. He sat.

He placed one hand into the slow current, palm open, and let the water decide what to speak. Pebbles shifted beneath his fingers. One of them caught beneath the crease of his thumb, a shard of black stone, smooth on one side and sharp on the other.

He lifted it and held it toward the morning. The sun caught its edge, revealing a red fleck beneath the blackness. It looked like a flame trapped inside coal. He turned it slowly, as if consulting it for advice and then returned it to the river with care. The river had not asked him to take it. He had only borrowed its story.

He was still, but not idle. Inside him there were questions that had never formed words, only sensations. Like the feeling of a bird just before flight, or the ache of a star that knew it must burn but did not yet know for what. He did not ask why. The wilderness had taught him that "why" was not a beginning. It was a wall. He was not a builder of walls.

From the edge of the tall grass came a hush, not from animal or wind, but from something unnamed. He did not flinch. He turned his head with the patience of one who listens more than he speaks. Between the stalks stood an olive tree, crooked in posture but in full leaf. Its trunk held scars. One, along the side, curved like a question.

The boy approached and placed his hand upon it. The bark was coarse, but within, it pulsed life, slow and deep. He leaned in and rested his forehead against the scar. "You remember," he whispered, not as a declaration but as a trust.

The tree did not answer in sound. It answered in scent. Its leaves brushed his shoulder, and he smelled earth warmed by memory. He saw himself not alone but remembered by things that were neither men nor beasts nor angels. Just the world, carved in dust and echo.

He turned away from the tree, not out of dismissal, but because he sensed something had begun behind him. On the slope beyond the river stood a rock outcropping, white and weathered, with cracks shaped like veins. He walked slowly toward it.

Each step sank slightly into loam. The air thickened, not with heat but with meaning. He knew this place was not sacred because someone declared it so. It was sacred because it never asked to be known. It only asked to be received.

As he reached the outcropping, he saw what the cracks revealed. Inside the stone were fossils, fragments of shell, flower, and bone. Not full forms, but hints. Echoes. Memory caught in mineral.

He placed his hand on the stone and closed his eyes. Something ancient stirred, not a spirit or a voice, but a recognition. He belonged here not because he was mighty, not because he was chosen, not because he understood anything. He belonged because he listened.

In the dark behind closed eyes, he saw fire. Not destructive. Not wild. It was a fire that warmed without consuming. A fire that carried shape without weight. Inside it he saw a figure, not tall, not fearsome, but cloaked in silence.

The figure knelt beside a river. It bore no face, only presence. And in its stillness, the boy felt the truth.

There are voices that do not cry out. They do not echo in thunder or command in flame. They wait. They wait like seeds beneath winter. They wait like stars whose light has not yet reached the eyes who will name them. These voices are not hidden. They are sacred because they refuse to be loud.

He opened his eyes and the world held still.

A bird landed near him, thin and grey with specks of white along its wing. It did not sing. It looked at him, tilted its head, and then pecked the soil gently. From beneath the soil, it pulled a thread, brown and thin, perhaps root, perhaps string. He watched and then whispered, "I will not ask you to speak. I will ask you to stay." The bird remained a moment longer, then leapt into the air, not in panic but with purpose.

The boy sat again and placed his hands on the earth. He closed his fingers around soil and felt it cool and grainy. He did not seek signs. He sought rhythms. He sought the breath of the wilderness—not to tame it but to be shaped by it.

He thought of his mother, not her face but her silence. The way she hummed without melody when she ground grain. The way she touched wood before cutting it. Her hands were strong because they asked permission. She had never taught him that directly. She did not need to.

The wind shifted.

He looked up and saw the sky change, not color but direction. The clouds did not move quickly. They expanded. As if unfolding to make room. The boy breathed in and stood.

He walked again, not toward anything but into it. The wilderness was not a test. It was not a trial. It was not exile. It was invitation.

He would walk until he heard what silence had carried all these years. Until he felt the echo not as a question but as a return. Until the name inside him spoke, not aloud, but through the way he touched the world.

He did not cry out.

He waited.

Chapter Eight - The House That Waits

The journey began not with footsteps, but with breath. The kind of breath that rises before dawn, when the sky is still deciding whether to speak.

The boy, now twelve years carried from the womb, stood at the edge of the encampment, watching the horizon fold itself into prayer. The Passover was near, and the caravan would soon gather. But he did not rush. He listened.

Each year, the path to Jerusalem was traced like a memory retold. His mother and the one who raised him walked with reverence, not out of obligation but out of rhythm. The boy had walked this path before, but this time the stones beneath his feet felt different. They did not resist his steps. They received them.

The wind moved through the olive groves, brushing against robes and branches alike. It carried the scent of grain and sandalwood, of dust and longing. The boy inhaled deeply, not to fill his lungs but to remember. He did not speak much during the journey. He watched. He watched how the elders leaned into silence when they spoke of deliverance. He watched how the children played near the wells, unaware of the weight their ancestors had carried.

Jerusalem rose before them like a question carved in stone. Its walls did not shout. They waited. The boy entered the city with the others, his eyes tracing the cracks in the pavement, the worn edges of the gates, the way the temple did not dominate but dwell. It was not a fortress. It was a breath held in architecture.

Inside the city, the rituals unfolded.

Lambs were prepared.

Prayers were lifted.

The boy stood among them, not as one who performed, but as one who received. He watched the priests move with practiced grace, their hands steady, their eyes distant. He listened to the chants, not for melody but for meaning. And in the pauses between verses, he heard something else, something older than liturgy.

The temple did not call him by name. It did not beckon. It simply did not release him.

When the festival ended, the caravan began to gather like a tide returning to sea. His mother and the one who raised him assumed he walked among the kin, laughing with cousins, sharing bread with friends. But he had stayed.

Not out of defiance.

Not out of forgetfulness.

He had stayed because the silence had begun to speak.

Three days passed.

His mother's voice cracked with worry. The one who raised him retraced their steps with trembling hands. They searched among tents, among alleys, among the shadows of the city. They asked strangers. They asked in silence.

And then, they found him.

He was seated among the teachers.

Not standing. Not preaching. Seated. Listening. Asking. His questions did not seek answers. They sought openings. And those who heard him were astonished, not because he knew, but because he understood.

His mother stepped forward, her breath caught between relief and rebuke. "Child," she said, "why have you treated us like this? Look, your father and I have been searching for you in great anxiety."

The boy turned, not startled, not ashamed.

"Why were you searching for me?" he asked. "Did you not know that I must be in my Father's house?"

Not because the words were unclear, but because they were too clear. The boy had spoken not as a son of lineage, but as a son of something older than blood. He had named the temple not as a place, but as a belonging.

He rose and walked with them.

He did not argue.

He did not explain.

He returned to Nazareth, obedient not out of duty, but out of love. And his mother, though confused, treasured all these things in her heart, not as answers, but as seeds.

But the boy had changed.

Not in stature alone, but in stillness. He no longer watched the world as a child. He watched it as one who had heard its breath. The temple had not taught him. It had remembered him.

Back in the village, the rhythms resumed. Grain was ground. Wood was shaped. The boy moved among them, his hands steady, his eyes distant. He did not speak often, but when he did, the words felt like echoes of something older.

He walked to the edge of the fields where the olive tree stood, the one with the scar curved like a question. He placed his hand upon it again. The bark was coarse, but beneath it pulsed life, slow and deep. He leaned in and whispered, "You remember."

The tree did not answer in sound. It answered in scent. Earth warmed by memory. The boy closed his eyes and saw the temple again, not its walls, but its silence. Not its rituals, but its waiting.

He saw the teachers, their robes heavy with tradition. He saw their eyes, wide not with disbelief but with recognition. They had seen something in him, not a prodigy, not a scholar, but a mirror.

He had not taught them. He had reminded them.

Chapter Nine - Where the Feather Landed

The boy walked beyond the almond trees, barefoot now, where the soil cooled his skin like water that never flowed. Behind him, the village pulsed gently, bread ovens breathed their morning warmth, whispers gathered like swallows under the eaves. Yet he moved away, not in rebellion, nor sorrow, but drawn by something older than words.

He did not intend to reach the river. It summoned without syllables, beckoning like a forgotten tune. When he arrived, the feather was waiting. Resting among reed and stone, it was not white, but a pale echo, almost the color silence would take, were it given shape. Slightly curled, as if the wind had once lifted it high, then released it with care.

He bent slowly, as if approaching a truth too fragile to name, and lifted it with two fingers. It didn't tremble. Nor did it resist. It simply met his hand.

Something passed through him, not thought, not memory, but recognition. The kind known only when shadow meets breath and both pause together.

He turned it once in his palm. It shimmered faintly, not from sun alone, but from some inner heat, like memory that had not yet been spoken. And he noticed, not for the first time, yet as if anew, that his fingers had calluses not from labor, but from holding things too gently.

There was no sound. Even the river seemed to hesitate.

He sat on a smooth stone and held the feather aloft. Light touched it differently, refusing to pass through cleanly, bending as if to glimpse its own reflection. A hawk circled far above. It did not cry, but tilted its wings subtly, as if witnessing.

Beneath him, the stone was warm. Not merely from daylight, but from time, layered with footsteps, dreams, and the ache of those who had once paused here. He closed his eyes.

A breeze moved past, gentle, then still.

"Am I still within the fold? Or have I stepped beyond the gate?"

He did not speak these words aloud. Yet something in the feather answered, not in movement, but in presence. It pressed gently against the unseen veil, the one between boyhood and becoming.

A wind rose, not fierce, but with purpose. It brushed his tunic, lifted a stray curl near his ear, and, in one gesture of grace, took the feather.

Not stolen.

Not lost.

Carried.

He stood as it floated skyward.

And before it fell again, he walked.

The boy moved farther along the stream until the trees thickened. Their bark bore marks, not of man, but of listening. Small grooves. Places where wind had lingered, where moss grew not downward, but upward, as if reaching. He touched one trunk and closed his eyes. It felt like skin, not in texture, but in memory.

Beneath his feet, stones gathered. They were not scattered but arranged, an ancient path, perhaps not made but remembered.

One stone bore a crack in the shape of a listening ear.

Another pulsed faintly with warmth.

He stepped carefully. The stones did not move. They received him.

A reed brushed against his leg, and he paused to listen to its whisper. It spoke of things that never shouted, of the moon's weight on still water, of footsteps that leave no sound.

Ahead, a fig tree arched over the path. Its roots gripped the earth like fingers around a secret. The fig tree did not greet him. It observed. Its leaves shimmered with a green so deep it echoed blue beneath their folds. He stepped beneath its branches and sat.

For a time nothing moved.

Then, softly, he traced the bark; patterns within patterns. A spiral that never closed. A shape like the feather's curve, drawn once and faded.

He whispered again, not words, but breath, "Memory is not what is kept. It is what returns."

As if stirred, the tree dropped a single fig. It landed beside him, and he picked it up. Its skin was warm, its weight precise, as though timed to fall not by gravity alone, but by choice.

He opened it, not to eat, but to see. Within, the flesh shimmered with dark red, almost violet, as if blood and night had shared a language.

He placed the fruit back on the earth and stood.

The wind was no longer soft. It carried scent, not of fig nor olive, but of salt and distance.

Somewhere unseen, a body of water stirred.

The boy followed.

As he walked, he remembered fragments,

His mother's song hummed not in joy, but in endurance.

The night he saw two stars collide and wondered if light could scream.

The moment his hand touched cold metal and knew it was crafted by someone who had never smiled.

He did not cry. He did not harden.

Instead, he became quiet in a way that invited presence.

A leaf, caught in the wind, touched his cheek. Its texture was coarse, as if the tree that bore it had known fire. The boy whispered, "The wilderness does not begin when one enters the forest. It begins when the forest enters us."

He arrived at a clearing. It held nothing, no structure, no altar, no names carved into stone. Yet it sang. Not aloud. But something ancient moved through it, like breath between stars.

He knelt.

The soil here was darker. Almost blue. It smelled faintly of iron and rain. He placed his hand upon it and felt a pulse. "You are not alone." The phrase did not come from voice, nor wind. It came from silence that had been waiting.

He did not ask who spoke. He did not need to.

He stood, and the hawk reappeared.

This time it cried out once. Not sharply. But with intention.

He watched it circle, then rise, until it became no longer a bird, but a memory of flight.

The boy turned and began the walk back, not toward village, but toward himself.

Chapter Ten – The Echo Beneath the Threshold

The wind had stirred the fig tree. It moved not like a storm, nor like a warning, but as if awakened by memory, a flicker of longing left behind by a breath. Leaves trembled with silver edges as the boy descended from the hillside, the place where solitude had found him and asked him questions in silence. The sky was bruised violet, a slow unraveling of the day's last intentions.

He was fourteen now, though the age itself felt less a number than a threshold - one that time had invited him to cross in silence.

He had sat for hours in the crevice beneath the cliff, a hollow carved by the patient hands of wind and time. There, stone and shadow had listened to him, though he had spoken little.

Thoughts bent toward the eternal in him, not as conclusions but as threads, unfinished, taut, humming. He had watched ants mapping journeys across the rock. He had seen the sun spill gold over the valley and vanish as though on cue. He had heard a distant owl declare something no one else would understand. And now, returning, he stepped toward home as though not fully returned.

The fig tree welcomed him with its tremble. He nodded in acknowledgment.

The threshold creaked beneath him, the rhythm of old cedar responding to a foot that had grown heavier with silence.

Inside, the Keeper of the Quiet Workshop was already at his labor. The hour was gold. Not the fierce gold of midday, nor the dim gold of temple coins, but the soft, forgiving hue that only appeared when the sun resigned itself.

He walked without haste, drawing wood from shadow, shaping it with reverent fingers. Resin softened the air. Dust rose in curls. In the hollow of this place, the sacred resided not in relics but in rhythm, measure, carve, join.

The boy paused at the door, not as a son, nor as an intruder, but as one who knew the language of thresholds. He had crossed one that day, though it left no trace. He had been eleven then, but something else pulsed behind his eyes, like starlight waiting to be named.

The Builder of Quiet Things moved without urgency. His hands, smoothed by years and softened by purpose, bent over olivewood beams. A frame began to take shape. Not ornate. Not boastful. But bearing the dimensions of comfort, of welcome.

In those gestures, the boy saw a liturgy. The wood received intention like a psalm. Each stroke of the plane, each touch of sand, each alignment of edge and joint, all carried memory. And not merely personal memory, but ancestral. Hands that remembered Eden without boasting. Hands that built not monuments, but mercy.

There was no greeting spoken. Not out of neglect, but reverence.

Words in such moments are like footprints on wet clay; they mar rather than clarify. So, silence presided, not as emptiness but as presence. It was the language that built stars.

The Guardian of the Threshold leaned forward, eyes tracing the beam. He shifted slightly, and the light caught the curve of his jaw. There was strength there, yes, but not the kind born from dominance. It was the quiet strength of one who bore without complaint, who protected without needing praise.

He Who Raised the Anointed One in Silence had no need for speech. His labor sang. His silence preached. The boy came closer, the scent of resin deepening. Time slowed, then paused. Somewhere, an olive dropped from its branch, unmissed but never wasted.

"The wind moved the fig tree," he said, as if offering a secret.

The One Entrusted with the Carpenter's Covenant stopped just long enough to lift the corner of his mouth. Not a smile, but a recognition.

"Then the fig tree must have longed for such a stirring," he replied, his voice quiet and shaped like the wood he held, steady, warm, unfinished.

Outside, dusk pooled like river water over stones. It collected in the seams of the valley, slid into cracks between rooftiles, curled beneath the eaves like a blessing with nowhere else to rest.

The boy took a slow breath, inhaling dust and dusk. His hand brushed a chisel left on the workbench. The feel of it startled him, its readiness, its weight. He didn't lift it. He simply touched it, then stepped back. He was not meant to carve what had not yet asked to be carved.

The Husband of the Hidden Mother stepped away from the frame, eyeing its angles. A small correction made. He lifted it toward the far wall, hanging it where tomorrow's sunlight would greet it.

That, too, was ceremony.

Not every priest wears robes.

In the flickering quiet, the boy drifted near the open doorway to their small garden. The fig tree stood there in silhouette, its branches now still. The wind had done its whispering. The boy felt the moment ripple through him, the idea that even trees could be stirred by knowing, by prophecy.

Later, the lamps were lit.

The Hidden Mother brought olives and bread in a woven cloth of indigo. Her movements were deliberate, quiet, gentle, the way the sea prepares tide. She said nothing of the boy's absence, nor did she ask what he had thought beneath the cliff. She knew. Not in specifics, but in the way only mothers know; through intuition, through scent, through dreams that arrive before the child speaks. She brushed a hand against his shoulder. It lingered just long enough to say, You have returned. And you are not the same.

The boy sat beside her. Not between them. As though the three were constellations suspended in deliberate orbit. The father's gaze met the boy's briefly. Nothing was exchanged, and everything was.

A pitcher of pomegranate juice caught the light. Clay warmed beneath fingertips. Candles stood tall and obedient, their flames unmoved by draft.

The bread tore gently.

Olives glistened.

The boy's thoughts stirred again, not loudly, but like birds shifting in a tree. He thought of the ants. Of the cliff's edge. Of the voice that had whispered nothing yet changed everything. He looked up. Through a narrow opening near the ceiling, a single star appeared, alone, pale, persistent.

And suddenly he wondered what stars remembered. Were they witnesses or participants? Had they chosen their place, or had they been placed? Was being seen their purpose, or seeing?

His breath caught slightly.

The Hidden Mother noticed, though she did not speak. Her fingers moved across the table like a prayer too soft to pronounce.

The Builder of Quiet Things took another bite of bread, his mouth quiet, his thoughts unwritten. Yet in that moment, the boy felt it, a presence not measured in words or gestures, but in density. The man radiated something, a kind of anchor that made flight possible.

The boy's gaze returned to the frame on the wall. It was ordinary in shape. But in its simplicity, it held everything, provision, presence, patience.

And blessings.

Always blessings.

Outside, the fig tree stood. No longer trembling. But changed.

Inside, the candles flickered, not wildly, but like they knew they were being watched. And in that silence, holiness lingered, not above them, nor beyond them, but within the cedar and oil, the bread and dusk, the fig tree and breath.

He Who Shaped Foundations reached for his cup. The One Entrusted With the Carpenter's Covenant looked toward the star. The boy blinked slowly. The Hidden Mother exhaled.

And the threshold remembered.

Chapter Eleven – The Edge of the Wilderness

The stones remembered him.

Even as he stepped lightly, even as his sandals left no defiant print, the wilderness, if it could be called that, offered recognition. Not of name. Not of age. But of longing. The kind that bleeds beneath skin without ever showing its wound.

He was fifteen.

There is no thunder in fifteen. No flood. No fanfare. Yet it is the year when longing grows limbs, and destiny whispers not in sentences, but in shadows cast by a fig tree now older by three summers.

He had come to the edge of it, not the wilderness as mapped by scroll or rumor, but the liminal terrain where childhood had finished speaking and manhood remained silent. The terrain breathed in folds, rocks curled against wind, acacia bowed as if remembering Eden.

The sky, thin as if fasting, held no obvious signs. No descending dove. No cleaving veil. Yet something in the air had changed. Not urgently. Not loudly. But completely.

He stood still.

Behind him, Nazareth hummed its ordinary songs, wood carved for tables, oil pressed from olives, laughter and argument mingling in stone courtyards. The Keeper of Quiet Workshops still shaped mercy into beams. The Hidden Mother still folded bread like prayer.

But the boy, soon to be a man, though not yet, had reached the edge.

The edge of hunger.

Of prophecy.

Of waiting.

And of a voice that was not his, not yet.

"A voice cries in the wilderness…"

But not here. Not yet. The cry belonged to another. One born of locust and honey, skin scorched by firelight and isolation. That voice had not yet echoed. But its silence hummed, an overture before revelation.

The boy sat upon a stone that had been warmed by late sun. The stone did not speak. But it listened. He closed his eyes. The wind, that old evangelist, moved across his skin like questions waiting for incarnation. Below the hill, a shepherd shouted something indiscernible, and a lamb trotted toward dusk. But none of it reached him.

His thoughts dwelt in layers. Beneath his ribs, uncertainty had made a home. A holy ache. Not confusion but pause. The kind that precedes the splitting of heavens. "It's not time," he whispered. Not to anyone. Not even to himself.

But the wilderness heard.

There was no path, but his feet made one, not through underbrush or thicket, but through the slow sediment of revelation. Each step sang softly against the soil. The wilderness did not resist. It received. He traced ridges of limestone carved by rainfall centuries before his birth. Beneath his fingers, the stone held memory, not of empires or miracles, but of erosion, the theology of patient change. Nothing in the wilderness happened quickly. And in that slowness, holiness nested.

He had come not seeking but listening.

Somewhere far off, a raven declared dominion. Closer still, a thornbush offered its clawed silhouette against the retreating sun.

He sat again. This time beneath an almond tree, its gnarled limbs bent in gestures that resembled prayer. In its branches, no fruit, only waiting. Waiting for the season. Waiting for rain.

Waiting, perhaps, for him.

"Prepare ye the way of the Lord."

But what was preparation if the voice had not yet been given?

He did not hear it with ears. Not yet. But the phrase hung in the air like dew, present, cool, incomprehensible. Its cadence was familiar, like a song sung once in dream. He knew the refrain.

Not its timing.

A single almond fell.

He did not reach for it. He watched it settle on the ground, unannounced and unafraid.

The edge of the wilderness was not made of beasts or tests.

Not yet.

It was made of restraint. Of divine pacing.

And of absence, not cruel, but deliberate.

He leaned against the bark. It did not yield. The wilderness never did. But it did not exile either.

It invited questions without insisting on answers.

He opened his eyes.

No one was coming.

And that was the point.

Solitude was not an absence to be solved, but a presence to be met. It did not offer conversation but offered clarity, slow and severe as sunrise over Sinai.

He stood again and walked.

His steps were unhurried. They did not challenge the wilderness, nor provoke its silence. They consented to it. And the dust lifted just enough to know he'd passed, then settled with indifference. Not denial. Just eternity's rhythm.

He paused before a crag that jutted into the sky like a discarded rib. Its shadow stretched long, distorting the contours of the pathless terrain. He traced its silhouette with his gaze and thought, not of Golgotha, not yet, but of the anatomy of isolation. How even rocks could seem to huddle against wind. How even silence could take shape.

A murmur pressed against his temples, not quite pain, not quite insight. Just pressure. A forming.

He sat once more. The almond tree behind him whispered leafless liturgies. Before him, open expanse. Above, nothing but the vast unresolved. Behind, a boyhood embalmed in wood shavings and morning prayers.

The ache inside him did not demand relief. It asked only to be named. But names were loud.

And today, he was listening for the quiet ones.

The sky flickered, not lightning, just the passing of a bird too high to be seen, casting a momentary shadow across his left cheek. He turned toward it instinctively, then did not pursue.

It was a sign perhaps, but not for now. Some signs are not meant to be read. Only remembered.

He reclined on one elbow and watched the wind rearrange the dust. It made no shape, no letter, no answer. Only movement. Only rhythm.

In his chest, a question nested, "Is destiny a summons or a surrender?"

There was no reply. But even the absence of one felt like instruction.

Below the hill, twilight had begun its slow conquest. Nazareth, hidden now behind slope and memory, glowed distantly in the way towns do when they forget the extraordinary in their midst.

He could hear it still, the clicking of pottery, the rise and fall of voices in dispute and affection, the water drawn from stone wells and poured into simple vessels. He loved those sounds. But they no longer contained him. He belonged here now. Not forever, but for the moment that precedes the moment.

A beetle crossed his ankle, deliberate and undisturbed. He watched its journey and felt the parable, movement not for spectacle, but for becoming.

He pulled his robe tighter. Not for warmth, but for anchoring. In the shifting hush of this landscape, the weight of fabric was a small tether to the known.

A fig tree stood several paces off, its leaves bronzing under the retreating sun. He walked to it and laid a hand upon its bark, which peeled in small memory shaped fragments. He did not pluck fruit. There was none. But he felt the longing of it in the branches, as if it, too, was awaiting a whisper.

"You are not alone," he said.

Not to the tree.

Not to the wind.

But to the silence, which sometimes needs to be told what it already knows. The fig tree gave no reply. But its posture softened, and that was enough.

He sat beneath it, knees drawn up, hands clasped loosely. He did not pray with words. Prayer, he had learned, was often a posture before it became language.

His breath slowed.

The wind stilled.

Night approached, not dramatically, but like revelation withheld.

In the darkening air, sound returned.

Not a voice.

Not a sign.

But a song. Distant. Barely formed. As if the stars themselves hummed the bones of it.

He closed his eyes and listened. It did not resolve. It did not crescendo.

It simply was.

A witness to his presence.

A branch creaked.

He looked up. The almond tree bore no fruit still, but one small blossom had formed. White, tentative, premature. He did not touch it.

Some things must be allowed to wait.

He rose again. This time, he walked with intention, not urgency, not certainty, but with the kind of motion that trusts uncertainty to be holy.

His feet traced a path the wilderness hadn't planned. But it welcomed him.

A nearby thornbush leaned into him, its spines catching fabric. He did not flinch.

There will be pain, he thought. But pain is not the antagonist. Only the tutor.

He looked skyward. Stars now emerged, first a scatter, then a congregation. No pattern. No prophecy. Just presence.

One star pulsed. He stared at it.

It did not move, yet something in him did.

A voice?

No.

An echo of one.

A yearning too ancient for syllables.

The fig tree was behind him now. The almond tree distant.

Before him, ridge, dusk, and an invitation.

He stepped into it.

Not because it was time.

But because time was beginning to make room.

Chapter Twelve – Of Thorn and Blood

He woke before color returned to the world. Shadows still clung to the soil, and even the sky seemed undecided, an argument between silver and bruised violet. The air lay heavy, damp with dream residue, and his skin bore the marks of what could not be touched.

A single breath unraveled the veil between sleep and waking.

The dream had come again, not as vision, not as comfort. It throbbed beneath his sternum like a second heartbeat. A vast desert sang in syllables too ancient to decipher. A figure moved within it, neither man nor beast, its body limned in flame, its voice quiet as sand. In its hand, a thorn, dark as obsidian, bleeding light.

Upon waking, he found his fists clenched.

He stepped barefoot onto the ground behind the dwelling, where river mist curled like incense. His shoulders felt too wide. His arms had grown thick with new strength, and he no longer walked softly. The muscles beneath his skin pulsed, neither rage nor calm, simply force awaiting direction.

The raven was there. It perched on a driftwood limb near the water, silent. Eyes like polished stone. In its beak, a thorn. Again. Not from any bush of this valley. It caught the light differently, black that glistened crimson. Without sound, the bird tilted its head, then dropped the thorn into the river. The thorn spun once. Then vanished.

The din inside his body had grown louder this year.

It began as sensation, then grew teeth. Thoughts surged with no anchor, desire, fury, hunger, all braided into an unnamable fever. Sometimes, when the world spoke too loudly, he pressed his hands against his ears until his breath became the only sound. He feared the noise might someday drown him.

His limbs yearned for motion, climbing, running, leaping beyond the hills. He rose before others, walked to places he'd never touched. His fingers trembled when idle. His spine felt too aware of itself. The shape of his body no longer matched the silence he'd once worn like wool. Even his voice betrayed him. It cracked when he tried to ask questions. It trembled when he offered blessing.

So, he spoke less.

And watched more.

The earth had changed. It wasn't just his flesh. The wind began speaking in fragments. The birds watched longer before flight. Stones carried heat even after dusk. Even the olive trees, once calming, now seemed too full, bloated with secrets. He smelled endings in the rain. The river sometimes felt like it was breathing.

One morning, after climbing the north ridge, he came upon a fig tree bleeding out of season.

No wound.

No hand.

Yet sap spilled from the bark like the tree had wept for something unnamed.

He touched it. Sweetness stung his fingertips, and he licked them without thought.

That night, his dream returned with thunder. The desert was bigger. The flame-being closer. Its thorn now glowed.

He woke briefly, remembering a moment with the old woman from the lower valley. She had no name, only wrinkles that folded the sky into her skin. As he passed her at twilight, she touched his chest gently. Just three fingers. No prayer. No blessing. "You'll need a stronger heart," she whispered. "One that bleeds without bitterness."

He had not replied. But her words followed him into sleep, into breath.

He fasted, not from tradition, not for ritual. He wanted to feel empty again, clean as early fog. But hunger did not purify this time, it stirred things darker. Thoughts clawed the walls of his mind. Flesh remembered sensations it had not yet known.

The eyes of others lingered now. Some in reverence. Some in question.

One girl walked past the olive grove, her shawl catching the light like flame.

He did not speak. But something inside him buckled.

His hands bruised a stone once, without meaning to. He had gripped it during prayer. When he opened his fist, it had cracked.

Another boy tried to provoke him, spat a curse that tasted of sulfur. He did not retaliate. But his breath grew loud. His jaw clenched until the other stepped away. No violence bloomed. Only heat.

He climbed higher mountains now, barefoot, bleeding on shale. It felt honest.

Once, during sleep, he felt his shadow move ahead of him. It turned. Spoke nothing.

But its mouth moved.

He woke up gasping.

The dreams became messengers. They spoke in riddles, of rivers under the stars, of a cave with a stone table, of a body pierced yet luminous. They did not explain. They invited.

One dream bled.

He woke with a red stain on his palm. It was gone by midday.

His mother began to watch him differently. Her hand lingered on his shoulder in the mornings. She asked fewer questions. Her eyes sometimes filled with knowing, and with distance. The women of the village whispered of passage, of body, of change.

They were right. But not complete.

This change was not only blood; it was cosmos entering bone.

He did not speak often now.

Words felt foreign, carved from timber too coarse to bear the weight of feeling. When he opened his mouth, even breath seemed uncertain, caught between silence and utterance. Language, once a friend, now watched him from afar, reluctant to come close. Yet inside, phrases bloomed. Not in any dialect he'd learned, but in patterns of sensation.

Heat became grammar.

Pain became poetry.

A tremor behind his eye spelled out hymns of resistance. His entire being had become a manuscript that no hand had written.

And still the dreams came.

Some offered torment, figures with no faces, limbs made of smoke.

Others brought sweetness, bare feet pressing into sand that whispered truth. Every night, something unnamable shifted beneath him, like stars cracking open.

Sleep, once a sanctuary, had become a battlefield.

Morning never brought rest, only evidence.

One dawn, he woke with a thin welt across his ribs. Not from any object. Not from movement.

Just... there.

Like the echo of a dream that he'd refused to remember. He stared at it in the dark.

Touched it lightly. And thought, This is mine.

He began visiting the stone basin carved into the hillside. It was neither spring nor stream, but a place where water gathered when the sky offered it. Most days it stood dry, its bowl dusty and dull. But when rain blessed it, he came barefoot, stepped in slowly, and stood until his body forgot everything but sensation.

One day, as he submerged his feet in that holy quiet, a thorn floated past, small, red, water polished.

He reached for it.

It pricked his thumb. Blood rose, round and deliberate.

He stared at the bead, how it held light, how it pulsed before falling. And in that moment, he felt something ancient curl in his throat, not sorrow, not rage. But recognition.

He climbed at night now.

To ridges the others feared.

Where the wind howled without permission.

Where animals moved unseen, not hostile, but never tame.

One night, he reached the high ridge and lay back on the stone. His chest heaved, more fullness than fatigue. Stars unfolded. Not gently. But like scars reopening. He opened his arms and let the wind strike his ribs, the cold reminding him of breath's fragility. Every inhale carried weight, every exhale a tremor of becoming. He whispered a phrase into the dark, no meaning, just rhythm. The mountain held it. Echoed it. Returned it in silence.

Later, he dreamt of a river beneath the earth. Flowing not with water, but with memory. He dove into it. It carried him to a chamber of bone. A table stood there, flat and cracked.

Upon it, one thorn. One feather. One drop of blood. He did not touch.

But he wept. And when he woke, the pillow beneath his cheek was damp. His fingers smelled of river.

The heat broke one evening. Rain came, not softly, but as a chorus of hammering. He stood beneath it without flinching, letting it baptize him into something unnamed. Around him, mud gathered in the hollows. Thunder split the air, and for a moment, the valley felt like a wound gasping open. He closed his eyes and whispered, "This is mine, again."

But this time the world answered, not with words, but with silence so deep it felt like language waiting to be born.

At twilight, he returned to the basin. It had filled to the brim. The thorn was gone. Instead, a feather floated on its surface, sleek, dark, iridescent. He reached out and took it. It didn't cut. It didn't bruise. It simply rested in his palm, light enough to vanish. And yet, it didn't. It stayed. As if held by something stronger than gravity. He looked at it and felt a phrase form in the pit of his stomach. Not to be spoken but carried.

Like blood in the veins.

Like memory in the bone.

He tucked the feather into his sash. That night, sleep came without fear. And dream didn't arrive like fire, but like quiet.

In the dream, the river of memory flowed again. He walked beside it. The chamber appeared, same table, same bone. But this time, something else lay between the thorn and the feather, A small, carved stone, smooth, grey, veined with gold. He picked it up and felt a warmth rise through him, not from the stone, but from within.

Not gift.

Not burden.

But calling.

He woke at dawn and knew. The silence he'd carried for years was not emptiness. It was preparation.

Every bruise, every breath, every prick of thorn had etched something permanent in him, an alphabet beyond speech.

He stood. Wrapped his sash tighter.

Climbed toward the mountain's edge.

And whispered one last phrase into the wind, "Let them remember me as the boy who listened."

The wind, for once, did not echo. It simply carried.

Chapter Thirteen - Wind Without Origin

The year bent low over the wilderness. In the borderlands between the tall juniper and the crumbling stone altars of abandoned shepherds, the boy grown into sinew and shadow watched the horizon without blinking.

Seventeen winters had etched their quiet arithmetic into his limbs.

The dust remembered each footprint he left as though it had been waiting centuries for him to pass.

They called him nothing. Not in contempt but in reverence. For in the tongue of the old hills, those who have no name walk nearer to the Eternal. He who carried the quiet did not answer when spoken to directly. His words came as fragments from dreams or half formed psalms lost in wind.

The elders no longer questioned him. They remembered the day he stood beneath the cedar and spoke of fire coming from within water. Since then, silence had become his crown.

He gathered wood with the other sons during twilight, though his touch was unlike theirs. Where their hands scrambled, his moved like a blessing. They laughed and threw stones to test each other's strength while he studied the flight of moths.

One dusk, as olive smoke rose in trails from their cooking fire, a serpent passed near his ankle. he did not move. It looked into his eyes and then slid away as if released from an oath it had once sworn.

The Anointed in Waiting sat on the riverbank most days, carving not names but symbols into the driftwood. Circles within circles. A single line spiraling outward into nothing.

The old woman who came each season to bathe her blindness in the water's edge murmured to him once, asking what the symbols meant. He did not answer but dipped a finger into the water and drew one in the slow current. She nodded, understanding beyond language.

At seventeen, the wind began to follow him.

Not merely as breeze, but as companion. It came from directions that had no name, from hills that had not yet unfolded. Sometimes it whispered into the reeds before he arrived, as though rehearsing.

One evening as he climbed the ridge where old bones had once been scattered as offerings, the wind stood still. Not absent but listening. He paused there, his silhouette thin against the indigo collapse of day and spoke a word so old that even the rocks shuddered to remember it.

In the village, mothers marked their doorframes with ash after he passed. They did not fear him. They feared what the world might do to someone so inwardly aflame. One father, bitter from harvest loss, muttered that the boy's silence was a curse. The next morning, he found his sick ox standing, healed. He wept for three nights beside its stall, unsure whether gratitude was permitted.

He did not write in scrolls. He etched into memory.

One day, the youngest of the shepherd boys followed him at a distance. They watched him kneel beside the old grave of the prophet who once sang to the wind. He pressed his forehead to the soil and remained there for hours. When he rose, the boy saw tears on his cheeks but no trace of sorrow. The air around him flickered, not with light but with some kind of anticipation, as though the wind now waited for permission to carry what it had learned.

Those who dwelled in the fringes, hermits with brittle teeth and eyes clouded by long solitude, whispered stories that would never be canon. They spoke of seeing him speak to trees in a language older than rain. They described birds circling him not in fear, but as students.

The Vessel of Fire did not perform signs.

His presence was the sign.

His body was lean now, shaped by fasting and slow practice of listening. He ate dates only when hunger reached his bones. He drank from springs that reflected stars more clearly than the heavens themselves. Once, while resting beneath a shattered dome where ancestors once read sky patterns, he watched the moon turn crimson. No one else noticed. But the stone beneath him grew warm, and a voice without throat spoke from within him, Prepare.

There were nights when he walked until the stars blurred. Not to arrive, but to be arrived at. He would speak into caverns where echoes refused to return. He saw visions, not in color, but in silence. A river running backwards. A child holding fire in his bare palms. A beast, horned and weeping, singing to a well.

Each morning, he washed his face with dew. Each night, he folded the corners of time into a prayer only the wind could read.

People began to call that year The Shifting.

Babies cried less.

Dogs howled at midday instead of midnight.

Bread rose without leavening.

The elders gathered once to discuss whether to ask him what it all meant. But none dared. Not from fear. From awe.

One day a stranger arrived. A man with eyes like burnt copper and hands scarred in places only thunder would understand. He carried no staff. No scroll. Just a voice like the third hour of night, hushed and holy. He did not speak to the young Vessel of Breath immediately. He waited three days, sitting beneath a fig tree that had not borne fruit in decades. On the fourth morning, it bloomed.

They spoke in silence. Not with signs or parables. But with wind.

No one heard their dialogue. But afterward, the wind turned. It no longer followed the boy. It began to lead.

Something had shifted.

He gathered a simple bundle. Not for journey, but for unburdening. He kissed the lintel of the house where he had once touched the stars as a child. He walked through the fields without saying goodbye, because goodbye was a word for those who did not understand eternity. He stepped onto the road toward the river. Not the one of bathing or cleansing. The one of becoming.

The sky watched. The dust recognized him. The wind, without origin, bowed.

He paused once more, where juniper leaned like sentinels and the dust held its breath.

Beneath the whispering cedar, now older, now listening, he placed one hand on the earth, not in farewell, but in offering. The serpent's path, the moth's flight, the prophet's grave, all stirred in the silence behind him.

And as the wind gathered in its new direction, the stars above did not speak, they opened.

Chapter Fourteen - The Breath Before the Descent

It was the eighteenth year of the Anointed in Waiting.

Stone warmed by sun.

Wind curling through almond branches.

Beneath the ridge of the old watchtower, he stood at the edge where dust faltered into silence. The Vessel of Breath had reached the season appointed, not by decree or temple bell, but by the turning within. No herald, no ceremony. Only the moths, drifting like pale hands through dusk.

His sandals, stitched by a quiet hand, were worn at the heel. The mountains had whispered once, when he was younger, of paths not yet drawn. Now, the whisper had returned, but it rose from within.

They said he had grown tall like the tamarisk. Those who knew him only from a distance spoke of how the wind seemed to linger near his cheek. But none could say what stirred within him, save perhaps the fig tree he passed each morning, though it bled not this season.

He had not spoken of what he saw in sleep, nor of the weight that now pressed behind the rib, where silence breeds shape. Even his mother, whose glance could sift stars from sorrow, had begun to wonder at the widening quiet between his words. When he spoke, it was no longer to explain, but to evoke.

In his hand, he carried a sliver of thorn. Not out of pain, but remembrance.

At the boundary where the river splits and joins again, the Bearer of Silence halted. The sun was lower now, angling like a question across his brow. Time here was neither line nor loop, but ripple. And he, a stone cast not by force, but longing.

He watched a serpent move across a patch of cracked clay. It paused beneath a reed, its tongue uncertain. And then it turned.

He wondered if even serpents questioned their path. He wondered if fig trees dreamed of fruit beyond season.

His eighteenth year was not an age. It was an echo.

Anointed, not by hands nor oil, but by the memory of winds that once remembered his name in syllables of flame.

He was the Son of Dust and Flame now. Not for what he had learned, but for what he had begun to unlearn.

That night, as the sky veiled itself in violet, he walked to the old olive grove, where silence pooled like rainless shadow. No one followed, not the brothers, not the neighbors, not the scribes whose eyes tilted in suspicion when he lingered too long near stillness.

Above him, three stars formed a crooked mouth. They did not speak. But they gestured.

A feather lay at the base of a weathered stone. It had not fallen by wind. It had been placed.

He bent and touched it. The wind responded, not with gust, but inhale.

And for a moment, it seemed the world remembered what it was before name and measure. Before the architects of order etched certainty into sand.

He whispered a phrase, "Let the wilderness call me by what I am not yet."

Not for others to hear. But for the wind to record.

The Vessel of Breath walked toward the southern edge of the hills where dust had hardened into amber stones. Each one caught light and shadow in alternating rhythms, as if the earth were practicing memory. He stepped without hurry. Time no longer felt like something to outrun, it moved with him, not behind nor ahead.

He passed the skeleton of a fig tree; its limbs gnarled into gestures of half-remembrance. Beneath it, a pile of ash. Not scattered but gathered. He knelt. Ran his fingers through the powder. It held no heat, yet his hand felt warm after touching it. He did not speak, but the wind shifted.

In the distance, a storm hovered. It would not arrive. It came only to watch.

He remembered a dream from his thirteenth year, a pool of obsidian, mirror-like, showing not his face, but three generations of his breath. Each figure older, each with eyes painted by silence. That dream returned now, not in sleep, but behind the eyes as he walked. With each step, the pool rippled.

A moth brushed his shoulder. Its wings bore markings that resembled a broken wheel.

The wilderness had not begun, yet it pressed into his skin.

He removed the thorn from his pouch. Held it flat on his palm. It had dulled since the river, but its shape remained perfect. Not beautiful. Not sharp. Just true.

He placed it into the hollow of an old stone altar.

Not as offering.

As memory.

The Son of Dust and Flame descended into the lower valley where thistle and bone shared root. It was there that stones carried their own breath, and the wind became a wordless companion again, less a follower, more a mirror. He walked at twilight, neither toward nor away, but into the fold of something that waited without name.

The trees grew sparse. Their limbs reached more than they shaded. One branch held a single feather, black, hollowed, and curled at the tip. He did not take it. He gazed until the wind moved it, then passed beneath as if to honor its gaze.

In the hollow of the valley, a fire burned where none had placed it. No ash, no kindle. Just flame, suspended over soil, flickering without smoke. He sat beside it, hands open, palms skyward. The flame did not warm, yet he felt heat from within.

He whispered. Not in a known tongue. Not with intent.

The fire leaned, listening.

And when it receded into nothing, it left behind a single stone. Grey-veined. Familiar.

He did not lift it.

He wept.

The air stilled, not the hush of nightfall or the muffled drift of snowfall, but a silence older than sound, as if the wind itself had paused to listen. There were no words in such stillness, only impressions, the sting of juniper in the lungs, the taste of stone on the tongue, the pulse of distance waiting in the dust.

The Anointed sat beneath a crescent of basalt, its shadow curling around him like a held breath. He had wandered ahead of the others, not far, just enough that the voices behind him blurred into birdsong and indistinct movement. His sandals rested beside him, damp with morning dew, while his feet pressed into the cool soil. It felt like memory, not his own perhaps, but something inherited, something whispered into clay before it became flesh.

He picked up a shard of obsidian lying in the dust, light as thought, sharp as grief. Holding it against the sun, he noticed how the light fractured into crimson and violet, prismatic slivers within opaque darkness. It was beautiful because it didn't pretend to be clear. Like the world, he thought. Like the Father. Like the desert.

He had dreamed of water the night before, not the lake, not the well, but a river with no banks, floating through starlight, endless and unfound. He could hear it even now, when he closed his eyes, a sound like breathing beneath breathing, gentle and persistent, winding through absence.

He remembered the dream and felt the tug of its unformed edges, a woman weeping with light in her hands, a boy who walked backward into the sea, a raven stirring cinders from the sky. These weren't stories, but fragments, like bones uncovered in the sand, still holding the shape of what once moved and spoke. Did the Father send such things? Or did the silence give birth to them?

In the distance, a juniper tree stood alone; twisted and wind sculpted. He felt drawn to it, not by curiosity, but recognition. Like it had known him before he arrived. As he approached, he placed the obsidian shard in a small crevice at its base, not as an offering, but as an answer to a question not yet asked.

Then came the breath, cold, wild, and first. It didn't arrive from any direction but seemed to rise from the ground itself, as if the wilderness had exhaled, and with it, a whisper not of words, but of being. It curled into his ribs and behind his eyes. It did not ask, "Are you ready?" It simply said, " Begin."

And he understood that the wilderness was not a place. It was a moment. A passage. A tear in the veil where time and origin stood naked, where he would not enter to prove something, but to remember something he had not yet lived.

He stood beneath the juniper. Closed his eyes. Felt the stone and thorn still waiting somewhere within the folds of earth. He lifted his hands, not as prayer, but as witness.

And in that stillness, something ancient whispered through the wind, no name, no command.

But recognition.

A fragment of light crossed his palm, soft, fleeting, half-known.

He opened his eyes and whispered it back.

Then stepped forward.

Chapter Fifteen - The Threshold Before Rivers Part

The morning was stitched in pale gold and ash blue, the kind of light that softened the mountains beyond the village and laid hush upon the road's dust. Birds had not yet sung. The fig trees along the eastern wall were still, save for one leaf that trembled as if recalling its origins.

Inside the workshop, the youth bent low over a warped table leg, eyes tracing every curve as if reading scripture carved not by words but by time. His hands moved with ritual. They did not hurry. They did not hesitate. When he sanded, the wood gave off a scent like forgotten incense, resin, and old memories, mingled with blood and cedar. A crack in the grain opened like a wound, and he placed his thumb over it gently, not to repair it yet, but to listen. To feel the shape of its suffering.

The door creaked once. He did not look up. He knew the rhythm of all who visited. Some came with voices. Some with silence. But silence could be loud when carried in grief.

Today, it was silence.

The man at the threshold clutched a small stool, legs split at the joints, one corner blackened by fire. His eyes did not meet the youth's but studied the floor as if the knots in the planks offered counsel. He placed the stool on the bench, not with reverence but apology.

"I found it near the well," he said after a long time. "It belonged to her mother. It's... It hasn't held for years."

The youth nodded. No word followed. Instead, he reached for his chisel, the one with the bronze handle, and began tracing the fractures, his movements slow and deliberate.

"I don't know if it's worth mending," the man added.

"All things that are handed down are already mended." the youth replied, voice quiet as a breeze slipping through olive leaves. "They break, yes. But breaking does not end a thing. It prepares it."

The man exhaled something between a laugh and a sigh, "You speak like a rabbi, but your hands speak more."

The youth said nothing. But he leaned closer to the stool, pressing the fractured leg into alignment as if coaxing the memory beneath it to rise again.

The youth worked in silence, save for the soft rasp of wood surrendering beneath the chisel's breath. Dust fell like ash, collecting in quiet rituals along the table. He did not speak for many minutes, nor did the man move. He watched, eyes fixed not on the repair but on the way it was done, as if the young artisan were not rebuilding furniture, but resurrecting time.

A child approached the doorway. Her hair was tangled with thistle and sky. In her small hands, she carried a ladder top, half split, rung missing. Behind her walked a mother, weary in stance, fingers wrapped around a basket whose bottom had unraveled.

"They say he repairs what remembers how to be whole," the child whispered to her mother.

"And what forgets?" the mother asked.

The youth looked up then, eyes meeting theirs, not with inquiry, but invitation.

He took the ladder top gently and laid it beside the stool, then gestured to the basket. The mother hesitated, as if ashamed of its frayed state. But he accepted it as one might cradle a wounded bird.

"Nothing forgets," he said softly. "Some things just need to be held longer."

The man who had brought the stool seemed stirred, as though he had remembered something not about wood, but about himself.

"I came here once, years ago," he murmured. "Brought a gate that refused to close. You fixed the hinge. I thought it was just carpentry then."

"It was," the youth answered.

"Was it?" the man pressed.

The youth paused. The chisel in his hand gleamed briefly in the morning light, then dimmed beneath the gathering shadow of midday.

"Wood remembers pressure. It remembers where it bent and how far. People do too. I only remind things how to hold again."

"And people?"

"People carry splinters deep," he said, voice now low, as if speaking to the grain itself. "But they still fit together."

The sun had begun its descent, pulling light into the west as if collecting coins from an unseen table. The village hummed in late hour ritual. Doors closed. Sheep bleated once before silence claimed them. In the workshop, the youth wiped a fragment of dust from the bench, eyes lingering on the repaired stool, the ladder top, the basket now rethreaded with care.

Then the shadow entered. No footstep announced it, no greeting. Just a figure, robed in travel worn linen, eyes rimmed with sleepless roads. He did not carry wood. Nor fabric. Nor metal. Only a gaze that asked more than time usually permitted.

"I've heard," the stranger said, "that you repair the broken."

"I receive what needs remembering," the youth replied, without turning.

"But what of the soul?" the man asked. "Its wood is invisible. Its breakage silent."

The youth placed a tool on the shelf, then turned.

"Have you brought yours?"

"No," the man whispered. "I no longer know how to carry it."

The youth stepped close, not in confrontation, but in recognition. He touched the bench beside him and gestured gently for the man to sit. It was not command. It was permission.

The man sat, and for a long time neither spoke.

Then the youth, voice soft as twilight, said, "In my earliest memory, I watched a sparrow mend its wing with its beak. It took days. Perhaps weeks. But each time it pressed against the broken part, it whispered not in pain, but in instinct."

"What was the instinct?" the man asked.

"To become what it remembered it could be."

"I cannot remember."

"You will."

The youth looked toward the open door, where the light had dimmed to violet. "When the fig trees bloom next, someone will knock at a door not built yet. And they will not ask for wood, but for presence. And I will go."

The man stared, breath caught, as though the air had braided itself with prophecy.

"You mean—"

"No," the youth interrupted gently, "Not yet. But the table I mend today will one day feed twelve who do not yet know each other. And the chair? It will break again. But it will be remembered. Not for its wood. But for the truth it held."

The man rose slowly, transformed not by answer, but by the permission to be unfinished.

"Thank you," he said, though no transaction had passed between them.

The youth nodded once.

And as the man stepped into the fading light, the youth remained inside, hand resting on the tabletop, tracing once more a small imperfection, no longer flaw, but map.

The village slept.

The repaired stool rested beneath the worktable. Not in forgetting, but in folded quiet. The ladder top leaned like memory against the far wall. The basket, now whole, hung near the doorway beside a linen cloth that once bore figs. Every repaired item hummed with a presence that exceeded its function, as though the act of restoration had pulled something eternal into the temporary.

The youth stepped out into the night, the air cool with mountain breath. Above, the stars whispered their familiar riddle, not yet answered, but not lost. He walked beyond the edge of homes, past the olive grove where children once played without knowing they'd grow into grief. Beyond the fig trees. Beyond the worn path that led to the river.

At the water's edge, he knelt, not as a seeker, not as a teacher, but as one listening for the echo between worlds. The river did not speak in words. It pulsed. It waited. And somewhere beneath its surface, a silence stirred that sounded like calling.

He placed one hand into the current. The water moved around his fingers, not resisting, not welcoming. Simply flowing. Carrying things unseen. He felt it then, not fully, not yet. But like the weight of a robe that hasn't been stitched, like a name that's known but not spoken.

A voice stirred within him, not audible, not foreign. Familiar as the timber he worked each morning, yet unfamiliar in its depth. It did not speak of tasks. It did not instruct. It simply waited, as if watching him remember.

He stood.

Looked upward.

And whispered, not to the sky, but to the joining place between breath and mystery, "They will come broken."

He did not say how many. He did not name the years. But he knew they would come, splintered in spirit, frayed in soul. The repairs he had made today would become shadows cast forward. The wood would return. Not as furniture. But as flesh. As ache. As hunger and healing.

And he would remember.

The hands that mend stools will one day touch blindness.

The fingers that shaped ladder tops will trace wounds not caused by hammers.

The heart that received a basket will multiply bread.

But not yet.

The youth turned from the river.

Walked back through the olive trees.

He entered the workshop one last time and placed the chisel beneath a folded cloth.

And as the stars continued their patient burning, the door closed behind him, not with finality, but with prophecy.

Chapter Sixteen - The Year of the Silent Pillar

Twenty cycles the fig tree bore fruit beneath his gaze, and still the silence grew stronger.

The winds no longer carried the scent of cedar.

In the house behind the olive grove, silence had settled like ash. Not mourning, not absence, something quieter. The villagers did not speak of the man who had shaped doorways and taught the boy to listen through grain. They simply began sentences with "when he was here," and let the rest fall like unfinished prayers.

Now, the youth stood alone in that house. Not just older. More still. The kind of stillness that pressed deeper than maturity, deeper than ritual. He carried the rhythm of another father now. One whose breath moved like wind between stars and whose silence guided birds across deserts.

In the early light, he rose to bake. No one taught him bread, yet it always rose, soft, golden, barely needing fire. A widow came each morning to fetch a loaf, saying little, except on one occasion when she touched his wrist and said, "When you shape things, even the bees know where to return."

He did not reply. Only smiled faintly and handed her the bread.

That day, he walked beyond the village. Past the place where fig trees broke through stone. Past the crooked stream that murmured secrets only swallows understood. There, beneath a twisted olive whose limbs curled like questions, he sat and carved, not wood, not stone, but the air itself.

He whispered.

And the tree straightened, slightly.

A boy watched from afar. He returned to the village and told his grandfather, "The Pillar bends light when he breathes." The grandfather nodded once, saying only, "He has reached the age when silence becomes a language."

The Elder's sandals still hung beside the doorframe, worn at the heel, threadbare at the strap. No one had touched them. Not out of reverence, but out of the strange truth that some things remain as they are when touched too often by silence.

A boy entered one morning, no taller than the window's curve, and asked to sit near the hearth. "My father says the Pillar is gone," he said, voice trembling with both sadness and curiosity. "But I see him in your posture."

The youth stirred the embers without reply. A fig had ripened early on the sill, though it was not its season. The boy noticed, "Did the fruit come because you were thinking?"

He touched the fig but did not grasp it, "Some things answer thought. Some answer longing."

The boy blinked slowly, "I want to be like you."

"You already are."

Later that day, he walked to the river, not for cleansing but for remembering. The current moved soft, the stones beneath it clear and warm. There, an old woman sat, hair white as salt, eyes bright as flame.

"You look like him," she said.

"I do not carry him," the youth replied. "I carry what he touched."

"Same thing," she murmured, and handed him a folded cloth. "He left this here last winter. It still smells of cedar and bread."

He received it as one receives a prophecy not yet spoken—folded, fragrant, full of instruction.

She did not ask him his name. She simply said, "The sky follows you like a student follows the sound of wisdom in a cave."

The river swelled just past the bend where the reeds grew crooked, too many moons had passed since its last quietness. The youth stepped barefoot into the shallows, not with purpose but with listening. There was a rhythm beneath the sound, something older than breath.

A stone flicked upward as he walked, revealing a fragment of charcoal. He knelt and touched it, eyes narrowing not with recognition, but remembrance. It bore the shape of a fingerprint, pressed into it long before fire hardened its edges.

A heron lifted from the far bank. Its wings cast a shadow that traveled across his chest like a garment being tried on. He did not look up. He whispered instead, "May I carry what did not break?"

The reeds answered by leaning.

From behind him, a small voice carried, "You walked like he did. Not into the river, but into its memory."

The youth turned. The boy had followed silently, fig still cupped in his palm. "I thought I'd lose the taste if I bit it," he confessed.

"That's how longing teaches," the youth replied, smiling softly.

The current pulled gently at the hem of his tunic. He stood still until the river released him.

Then, with a nod toward the boy, he spoke, "It's time to gather the sandals." Not to wear them. But to remember how distance is measured, not in steps, but in how slowly silence lets go.

The sun had begun its slow withdrawal, spilling bronze across the hills as though reluctant to leave. In the village, voices quieted into the grain of things, footsteps softened, pottery clinked like memory. Even the dogs lay still, sensing that sound itself was folding into rest.

At the workshop's edge, the youth sat with the cloth the Elder had once left, now unfurled across his lap. It bore a faint stain, oil or blood, no one remembered. But the mark pulsed gently, like something that had once spoken and chose now to wait.

He did not move quickly. This was the hour for listening, not mending. The fig from earlier rested untouched beside him. It had begun to split gently, revealing its insides without invitation.

Across the way, the child stood watching, half-bitten fruit still in hand. He did not speak. But his gaze was steady, as if observing not the youth, but the space around him, the way the light touched his shoulders, the way dust chose not to settle on his feet.

The boy whispered to no one, "He does not cast a shadow at this hour. He carries it instead."

And just then, a breeze passed through the workshop, stirring wood shavings into brief motion. The sandals shifted slightly on their peg, not falling, not swinging. Just enough to remind the room that presence is not always anchored by bodies.

The youth exhaled, slow and deliberate. Not weary. Not worried. But as if breathing had become his covenant with all things air, grain, memory, ache.

Dusk pressed in fully. The stars had not yet arrived, but they were watching. The hills held their lines more softly now, blurring into one another like stories retold by firelight.

And at the edge of all this, he rose, not for ritual. Not for departure. But simply because dusk had given, what it came to give and now waited to be met.

That night, the wind carried a scent not known to season. Ashwood and bread, tempered by fig leaf and oil. It drifted into the youth's room as he folded the cloth once more, placing it beside a hollow carving the elder had begun but never finished.

He touched the hollow gently. Not to complete it. But to remember that some things are beautiful because they remain unfinished.

The sandals still hung.

He took them down, not to wear, but to place upon the table.

Outside, a branch snapped underfoot. Not threat. Not accident. Just the sound of someone walking as if their step knew how to echo. The youth looked toward the open door and saw no one.

But the air had changed. As if someone departed long ago had returned, not in form, but in recognition.

He whispered then. Not with voice, but with gesture. He traced a line in the dust around the sandals. A circle. Then placed a fig leaf within it.

"In the years he walked," the youth murmured, "he taught the grain to bear weight not with resistance, but grace. He taught me that pressure is not the enemy of purpose."

The stars above flickered. One fell. The youth did not flinch. He watched as it traced a brief arc toward the east, toward the olive tree that had straightened.

He remembered something once spoken by the elder when shaping a threshold beam, "Every doorway is a decision between memory and mystery."

That night, the youth dreamt.

He stood upon a hill made of chisel shavings. Beneath him, the earth hummed with names he had never learned. Above him, the sky sang, not with sound, but with rhythm. A single phrase unfolded within him, older than time, "You are held by more than the hands that shaped you."

He awoke before dawn. The sandals were gone.

In their place, a pair of footprints in wood dust, leading nowhere. Or perhaps, leading inward.

The youth stepped into the blue hush before dawn, sandals echoing now not on stone, but on memory.

He carried nothing. Not bread, not blade. Only the fragrance of cedar and a single thread of wool from his father's last cloak twined around his wrist like a vow not spoken aloud.

Past the olive grove, the wind moved as if cued by longing. It caressed the trees not to disturb them, but to remind them they were seen.

He walked east, where the sky turned from charcoal to silver. A valley opened, a shallow cradle of land shaped not by time but by intention. There, birds gathered without cause. A murmuration paused overhead, their silence louder than prophecy.

The youth knelt. Not to pray, but to listen.

Beneath him, the ground held warmth. A hearth remembered. He pressed his hand into the soil and whispered, "He taught me to build things that did not collapse in winter."

The sun broke the ridgeline.

Its first light landed not upon the youth, but upon the distant beam of a gate long removed. There, a shadow etched in wood, still visible, still shaped like two hands reaching toward each other.

The boy rose.

Behind him, the wind braided itself with light.

He did not look back, not out of defiance, but trust.

He whispered once more, this time with breath, "In his silence, God taught me to speak."

Then walked on, into the wilderness.

Chapter Seventeen - Sand That Remembers Rain

He had walked through twenty-one seasons of planting and dusk, yet the ground still did not call him by name. It spoke instead in texture, in the grain of wind between fig leaves, in the way sand shifted beneath footsteps that asked permission.

The high plain was still. Stones lay like sleeping elders, waiting for the sky to change its mind. Overhead, the sun hovered as if not yet committed to descent, and the wind moved sideways through saltbush.

He did not seek shade. He stood in full light, neither as offering nor defiance, but as one learning how dust listens.

To the east, a ravine split the earth like a wound healed without stitching. He stepped toward it. Beneath each footprint, the ground breathed, a slow release of heat and memory. He knelt there, where the stone curled back like the edge of an old scroll.

There was no parchment. Only the trace of something written in absence. The wind passed once, then paused. A shape stirred beneath the sand. A shard? A bone? A forgotten syllable?

He reached down, not to take, but to touch.

And the ground replied, not in sound, but in fragrance, a faint trace of rain fallen long ago, when the world still knew how to weep without reason.

The ravine deepened, not with descent, but with memory. As he walked, the air changed. It began to taste not of dust, but of something older, mineral, fig, iron. The wind slowed, curling inward like a hand drawing fire into its palm.

There, beneath an outcropping of basalt, sat a man cloaked in the color of twilight. He did not rise. He did not speak. Yet everything near him had shifted, the stones bore warmth where shadow should live, and a single sprig of wild hyssop bent toward his feet as if seeking pardon.

The younger figure stepped forward. Not toward, but beside. He sat, mirroring the posture, without knowing why.

"Some things do not announce themselves," the older said. His voice was low, shaped like gravel smoothed by song.

"They arrive only where silence is deep enough to receive them."

He nodded slowly.

"Is that why you waited here?"

"No. This is not waiting. This is remembering."

Between them lay a circle of sand drawn thinly with bone. Inside it, two stones faced each other. Nothing more.

"This line," the younger said. "It's a threshold?"

"It is a conversation. Between what passes and what stays."

The hyssop shifted again, curling inward. A small bird landed just outside the circle. It did not sing. It watched.

"Tell me," said the younger, eyes steady. "What does the sand remember?"

The elder drew breath, slow as twilight.

"It remembers the softness of water. And the weight of footsteps that did not belong to beasts.

It remembers when stars lowered themselves to speak, not to guide, but to weep.

It remembers pain without blood. And joy without sound."

A silence fell like dusk on temple steps.

"How do you know?"

"I was there."

"Not here," he clarified. "But in the ache it carries. I shaped a table once from cedar split by thunder. But the thunder never made sound, it only changed the wood's breath. That is how I knew you would come."

He bowed his head. Not in understanding, but in reverence.

The sky had begun its slow turn toward evening, yet one star had arrived early, burning faint green, pulsing thrice before fading. It did not blink. It recited.

The younger whispered then, not in speech, but in gesture. His hand moved over the sand circle, not disturbing it, but listening. Beneath his touch, the stones warmed.

"You carry more than the river's silence," the elder said. "You are shaped by things that have not yet spoken."

He looked up. Light shifted over his shoulders without landing.

"Then let them speak," he said.

The wind quieted as they entered the cave, not ceasing, but condensing. It became a pulse, then a hum, then a breath beside the ear. The rock swallowed sound. Even their footsteps dared not echo.

The elder reached the far wall, where markings shimmered like mica, carved not by blade but by longing. Glyphs bent inward, folded like fig leaves in late dusk. Some glowed faintly when passed; others pulsed when watched.

"These," he said, "are not written to be read. They are breathed to be remembered."

"By whom?"

"By what waits beneath the silence of stars."

He stepped forward, not touching, only observing. One marking bore the shape of a tree bending in wind, not broken, just listening. Another held the spiral of two seeds stitched by flame.

"This one speaks in pairs." said the elder, gesturing to a coiled figure. "It sings of things born twice - once in flesh, once in ache."

He turned.

"And this?"

The glyph curled like a whisper dissolving in water.

"That one doesn't speak. It remembers the time before speech."

A silence stirred, heavier now. Not oppressive. Weighty, like stone waiting to be named.

The younger reached toward the spiral, hand hovering.

"You feel the echo?" the elder asked.

He nodded.

"That means it has chosen you. Or perhaps you have returned to it."

A beam of light slipped through the cave mouth, angled like a finger pointing down an unseen path. It landed on an alcove hidden behind folded stone. Within lay something wrapped in fig bark and thread dyed with iron ash.

The elder didn't touch it.

"It has waited through twenty-one passings of seed and sky. Not for a reader. For a listener."

He stepped forward and lifted the bundle. It unwrapped slowly, like a wound choosing to open.

Inside, not parchment.

Not scroll.

Wood.

Polished smooth, etched in flame marks. No words. Only patterns that moved when looked at long enough, spirals, stars, waves, bones. Breath.

He placed it in his lap.

"This is not a message," he whispered.

"It's a memory carved by one who dreamt in matter."

The elder sat beside him.

"Read nothing. Let it speak."

He closed his eyes, the carved glyph still warm in his lap. The breath he drew was no longer from the cave, but from a space beneath vision, where memory folds into rhythm, and rhythm becomes doorway.

Sleep came like dusk falling on an altar. Not quickly. Not gently. With reverence.

And what followed was not dream, but architecture.

He stood beneath a canopy of fig leaves, though no tree was near. The earth beneath him was wet, not with water, but with remembering. Each step pressed into the soil, and the soil replied in color, umber, ochre, pale flame.

Ahead, a figure walked, not taller, not smaller, but earlier. Not clothed, but covered, by light, by wind, by something that knew how to carry intention. The ground did not respond to his steps. It leaned toward them.

He followed without knowing.

They reached a clearing shaped like a breath held too long. In its center, a single stone split down the middle by nothing visible. The air around it shimmered, as if time refused to settle there.

The figure turned, not fully, just enough for presence to be felt.

"You hear differently now," the voice said.

Not masculine. Not feminine. Not echo. Just true.

"I see what speaks without voice," he replied.

"And what does it say?"

"That memory is older than creation. That rain was not invented, it was remembered."

A pause.

"Then you are ready."

The stone pulsed, once. A color that had no name poured from its crack.

"This place is not held by soil," the figure whispered. "It is held by ache. The kind that forgets why it began but never stops unfolding."

He stepped toward the stone.

It did not resist.

The stone split farther, but not by fracture. It unfolded, like breath in reverse. Inside, there was no relic. No flame. No blood.

Only air.

But this air sang.

Not loudly. Not with melody. It sang like dust caught in light, revealing rather than announcing. A hum so deep it touched the chest before the ear. The younger stepped closer. The older remained still.

A gust from nowhere scattered fig leaves across the clearing. The wind had returned but changed. It carried no scent yet held recognition.

He reached into the opened stone, not to grasp, but to bless. His fingers did not disturb the air but aligned with it. Beneath his touch, the hum shaped itself.

Words came, not as speech, but as pattern.

"Where flesh begins to remember, light returns."

"Where silence no longer waits, fire softens."

He spoke to them, not by will, but because they had always waited within him. And once said, they did not linger, they joined the wind and disappeared.

The figure from before, neither crowned nor veiled, stood again in the clearing. This time without distance.

"You walk now not toward a calling," the voice said, "but inside it."

"Then where is the threshold?"

"It walked behind you. And now carries your shadow."

He did not cry.

He did not speak.

He knelt.

The fig leaves settled.

The wind returned to stillness.

And beneath his palm, the air cooled, the earth breathed, and the stone whispered one final phrase, carved not into matter, but into ache,

You are not born into the world. You are remembered by it.

Chapter Eighteen - The Woman Who Braided Silence

She lived beyond the ridge, where fig trees tangled with wind and the river forgot its name. Her dwelling, more ruin than shelter, bore no threshold, only a curtain of woven reeds that moved not with wind, but with memory.

He, who is twenty and two, arrived barefoot. Not in poverty, but in reverence. Dust clung to his ankles like a prayer that had never been spoken aloud. His presence disturbed nothing. Not even the sparrows watching from the almond limbs.

She did not rise when he entered. Her eyes, pale with age and unwept sorrow, flickered once toward him, then returned to the braid she was unbinding, a coil of silver and dusk woven together, tied with fig bark thread. It fell slowly into her lap, as if time were a garment.

He sat cross legged without speaking. His hands bore no offering, but his silence did. The kind that had shape. The kind that had walked far.

"I braided her hair the day before the vow," she said.

He did not ask who.

"She was younger than most. And older than any. Carried quiet like other girls carried linen."

The wind passed over the fig trees. One limb bent without cause.

"She did not cry. She did not smile. But her breathing trembled, and she asked me, only once, if obedience was the same as love."

The braid slid farther apart. It split into three strands on her lap.

"She wrote a word in ash. Just one. I watched her fold it into a clay vessel and bury it beneath the fig roots. That vessel is still there. I can feel it. The fig tree leans when no wind moves."

He lowered his gaze. His silence did not comfort, it communed.

"She feared being remembered only by her silence," the woman said. "But I told her silence remembers us far longer than names."

The reed curtain stirred.

"She will live again when someone speaks not her name, but her question. You may be that voice. Or you may only be its echo."

The strand of silver fell from her lap onto the clay between them.

"She braided silence because she had no thread for grief."

He placed one hand on the earth. Not to ask. To listen.

The fig tree groaned once. Then stilled.

She motioned toward the fig tree, not urgently, not even deliberately. As though the tree had already heard her.

"I buried it not with grief," she said, "but with forgetting."

Her voice fell like olive leaves. Slow. Each syllable seasoned by time, not sentiment.

"The vessel was clay, smoothed by my own breath. Inside it, ash from a fire that no longer smoked, and one word pressed into its center, not scratched. Pressed."

She stood. He remained seated, watching how the light did not touch her fully, only glanced across her shoulder, as though wary.

The grove extended beyond her hut, tangled with vines and memories too old to name. She walked without aid, each step familiar, not rehearsed, remembered.

He followed. His feet met hers in silence, neither leading nor lagging.

The fig tree they approached bent not toward sun, but toward earth. Its limbs held the posture of one who'd listened too long. Beneath it, stones arranged in a circle, twelve, but not equidistant.

"This is where she hid the vessel," the woman said. "But the hiding was not concealment. It was an offering to time."

He knelt. Not in supplication, but in alignment.

"She asked me to remember it only when a fig tree bent without wind. That happened five seasons ago. I returned then, but the vessel had changed."

The earth shifted, faint, almost imperceptible.

It had grown darker. And inside the vessel, the ash was no longer cold. It pulsed, as if waiting.

She placed her palms on two stones. Her fingers trembled once, then steadied.

"This circle was drawn by her breath alone." She exhaled twelve times, naming rivers, each one a current drawn from the circle of her breath.

He closed his eyes. The ground beneath him was not still. It remembered.

Then she began the rite.

No flame. No chant. Only gesture. She lifted the braid from her lap and scattered its strands among the twelve stones—one coil per river named. As she placed them, the tree groaned again.

She bent down and touched the soil.

Each strand of hair sank slightly, accepted by the earth as if it were returning home.

Then she sat again, knees folded, back straight. She placed the bowl of rainwater between them, just as she had done years ago.

He reached in and lifted the single thread.

It clung to his fingertip.

She whispered, but not to him. Not to the air.

To the silence.

And the silence answered, not in sound, but in memory.

The silence in her face had become something else, no longer the hush of unspoken grief, but the stillness that cradles knowing.

She lifted the bowl slightly, as if its ash had weight again, and stared into the threads he had placed there. Her voice arrived like breath between stone, "You are not the first who has come through here with stillness in his eyes. But you are the only one it did not frighten."

Her gaze held him with peculiar fire, not the heat of judgment, but recognition, a quiet ache that had lived long in the folds behind her brow. She raised one hand, not to touch him, but to shape the air around his face, tracing lines the world hadn't drawn yet.

"I saw you once," she said, "when I was a girl by the eastern hills. A fig had broken in my hand. And I looked down. There was a voice in the juice, and it told me not your name, but the ache you would carry."

He did not answer.

"I braided that ache into silence," she murmured. "Years and years. Until silence became the shape of waiting. I did not know for what."

The bowl shimmered with something unspeakable, memory that wasn't hers, a wilderness not yet walked. He reached forward and gently placed his fingertip into the center of the ash. A wind that wasn't wind stirred, and for one breath, the room felt like it remembered something ancient and unfinished.

Her hand, still hovering near the bowl, began to tremble, not with age, but with the weight of return. The thread he had lifted now rested again in the rainwater, pulsing faintly. She did not touch it. She simply leaned closer, her voice nearly inaudible.

"I was told once," she said, "that memory, when braided, holds the shape of the one who will unbraid it."

The silence between them bent like light passing through oil. He did not speak, but the air around him shifted, as though the earth itself had recognized him.

She turned her palms upward. Her scars, faint and crosshatched, formed patterns that mirrored the threads in the bowl. She looked at them, not in mourning, but in witnessing.

"There was a night," she continued, "when I dreamed of a figure walking through sand without leaving prints. He passed by the fig tree, paused, and whispered into it. The tree bent. Not from miracle. From memory."

Her lips quivered. The words seemed to stretch through decades.

"I woke and found fig leaves at my door. I did not own a fig tree. I knew then, he was coming."

He raised his eyes, and the room responded. A coil of dust lifted, spun once, then stilled.

"The ash in the vessel was not hers alone," the woman said. "It carries the ache of those who asked questions too old for answers. It pulses for them."

He reached toward the bowl again, and for a breath, the thread wrapped around his fingertip on its own, as though drawn to him not by gesture, but by recognition.

She watched it spiral. A single tear crept across her cheek and did not fall.

"You are not who she hoped for," she said softly. "You are who she knew would come."

Then she spoke the final words of the rite. Not to him. Not to silence. To the unbraiding.

"The ache becomes breath. The breath becomes thread. And the thread becomes the one who does not fear the fig's question."

The room grew still.

Outside, a fig leaf fell without breeze.

The rite had remembered him.

He did not stand when the rite concluded. The thread still circled his finger, not as adornment, but as weight. Beneath him, the twelve stones, placed by breath alone, seemed to hum in quiet accord.

She leaned forward and placed her hand atop his.

It was not a gesture of comfort. It was transfer.

"I once saw her enter the fig grove at twilight," she said. "She bent to the soil and whispered three words the wind forgot to carry. I do not know what they were. But the tree bent. And I knew it had heard."

He closed his eyes. And in the stillness, something deeper than vision emerged.

The clay vessel, long buried, long pulsing, spoke. Not aloud. Not in symbol. It released what it had held for years, the sound of a question never asked because it would fracture the world to answer.

He did not speak. He placed the thread back into the bowl, and where it landed, the rainwater shimmered, then stilled.

Then he reached toward the earth and moved one stone. Just one. The twelfth.

Where it had sat, the soil held a spiral.

Not carved. Not pressed.

Formed by waiting.

She gasped, but quietly.

"That is the mark she made," she said, voice barely more than breath.

He nodded. No vow. No miracle.

Just presence.

The tree bent farther. A fig dropped, split on stone.

Its juice bled into the spiral.

He reached down and touched it, not with finger, but with palm.

And the earth beneath groaned once, like memory completing its orbit.

Then nothing.

But it was not absence. It was arrival.

He stood at the edge of the grove; one palm still marked with fig juice and ash. The old woman did not rise, but her braid now lay fully unbound, three strands soaked with rainwater, haloed by stone.

He stepped from the twelve circle slowly, and where his foot fell, the earth did not stir, it received. Quietly. As if it had been waiting centuries for that weight.

The fig tree behind them, bent yet resolute, released one final leaf. It drifted, not down, but across, gliding along the spiral etched in the soil.

The woman watched the leaf settle. Her fingers moved toward her lap but stopped. She did not reclaim the thread. She did not reclaim her voice.

Instead, she looked to his back.

There, just above the right shoulder seam of his cloak, she saw a shape woven in dust, faint, nearly imperceptible. A braid. Three lines twisting once, then parting into wind.

No thread. No mark.

Just the memory of having once touched a silence that would become word.

She did not speak. There was no need.

He walked on.

The twelve stones remained. The bowl remained. The ash would remain until rain carved it back into forgetting.

But the fig tree knew.

It would bend again.

By dusk the stones had cooled. The bowl remained, untouched yet changed. Rainwater held the thread, but the ash had drawn inward, curling toward the center as if forming a word no alphabet could hold.

She sat alone now.

The braid had dissolved, scattered across soil that remembered too much. Her knees ached, but not from age. From arrival.

He had gone, quiet as he came. No farewell, no prophecy. Only a gesture.

She looked to the place where he had placed his palm. The fig leaf still lay folded into the spiral, and beside it, pressed into the soil, something shimmered faintly, a symbol not carved, but emerged. Not left. Realized.

Three lines, braided once. Then unbraided into silence.

She touched it.

A pulse moved through her.

Not pain. Not joy.

Recognition.

The ache she had carried for decades, unspoken, buried beneath hair and earth, had turned. Not into healing.

Into witness.

She whispered into the dust.

"He was the question."

And somewhere in the grove, a bird took flight, not from fear, but from fulfillment.

She did not rise when dusk settled. Her braid lay unraveled across the twelve stones. In the bowl, the rainwater held still. Only the thread stirred, twisting once, as if listening.

Her fingers moved to her lap, where they once knew rhythm. But tonight, they did not braid. They remembered.

In the far hush of memory, she saw herself again, young and unbraided, crouching beside a fig sapling that had bent though no wind passed. She had carved a single line into the soil that day, a mark without meaning, only ache.

Above her, the older women sang their consecration chants, braiding one another with laughter and oils. She had not joined them. She had taken a fig leaf and written three words with its stem across her palm.

One she forgot.

One was forgiven.

One she never spoke.

That night, she had looked into the sky and asked nothing. Yet something answered. A wing-shadow, a groan of limb, a silence that reached backward.

And now, here, beside this grove, beside this thread, she knew.

He had walked into the shape of her question.

Not as son. Not as messiah.

As reply.

She lowered her hands, the memory blooming like scent between stones.

Then she spoke, not with voice, but with breath.

"This is how silence remembers," she mouthed.

And the fig tree leaned once more.

The bowl rested lightly in her palms, no longer sacred, no longer simple, just what it had always been, the place where silence made its home.

Outside, the fig tree held its bend. The moon skimmed its canopy and cast silver across the thread, now settled like a question no longer waiting for answer.

She looked once toward the path he had taken. It did not remember footprints. Only presence.

Then she breathed.

Not to survive.

To remember.

And the earth listened.

Chapter Nineteen - House of the Whispering Bones

The village lay beneath the slope like a prayer forgotten mid recitation. Bethany, its olive trees bowed, its doors silent with the weight of mourning. Stones lined the path not in symmetry, but in sorrow; they had seen too many griefs to remember names.

He approached alone.

Not with entourage, not with proclamation. No staff carved with lineage; no garment dyed in sacred thread. He came dressed in the humility of one who has walked many circuits of the sun, three and twenty perhaps, though none asked. His eyes held the hush of stars seen from desert peaks, and his voice, when it emerged, would sound not as thunder, but as breath between sleeping mouths.

At the well, she wept.

Miriam, sister to the youth who died too soon. Her tears did not fall freely; they clung to the edge of her eyes, thick with doubt, with rage, with tenderness withheld. When he drew near, she did not look up. The air around him stirred but did not demand.

"You have come," she said, not as greeting but as accusation.

He nodded without sound.

"They said you travel like mist," she murmured. "That grief moves toward you as a tide moves toward moonlight. Did you come to stir the dead?"

"I came to listen," he said.

"To whom?"

"To the bones beneath linen. They do not sleep. They whisper."

She turned then, fully, her face unveiled. Her eyes searched his face for the echo of a name the villagers dared not speak aloud.

"You look like wind carved by mercy," she said.

"I am only what silence allows," he replied.

And together they walked toward the house, its walls thick with waiting, its door untouched since breath left her brother's lips.

The threshold did not creak. It received them.

Within, the body lay in the upper chamber. Linen wrapped, herbs pressed. The air still held scent but no spirit. The room was not a tomb.

Not yet.

He placed one hand against the wood. The grain pulsed faintly. Not with magic. With memory.

There was no sound inside the chamber. No scraping of wood, no stir of oil lamps. Only the hush of linen, pressed against skin that no longer knew warmth. The body of the youth had already begun its return to the earth, sweet spices clinging to him like memory, his lips sewn with light by mourning hands.

The stranger stood near the threshold.

He touched nothing.

Miriam, still veiled, lingered at the doorway, eyes wide but silent. Her grief had calcified, not fresh, not weeping, but dry, like forgotten fruit left on the branch after the season had fled.

The figure walked forward, not toward the body, but toward the silence that surrounded it. His presence did not pierce the air, it settled it, as if even the dust longed to listen.

He knelt beside the bier.

Laid his palm against the cedar board.

Closed his eyes.

There was no invocation. No name of God, no rending of veil. Only breath. Slow, steady. The kind that remembers what it feels like to be born.

The silence cracked.

Not loud. Not seen.

But Miriam drew a sharp breath, her fingers clutching at the braid she hadn't touched since the death.

His hand hovered now above the chest of the youth, fingers splayed, not commanding, not conjuring. Waiting.

Then his lips parted.

He spoke, not a spell, not a miracle.

He said the youth's name.

Once.

Softly.

And the linen stirred.

Miriam gasped. The oil lamp flickered. The stranger remained still.

Again, the linen moved, this time unmistakably. A wrist twitched beneath wrappings. The chest rose. Shallow, uneven.

Then….

the boy coughed.

Dry, weak. Like a root remembering rain.

The veil between silence and breath was broken.

He did not speak again.

Not to Miriam. Not to the walls.

Only to the youth, now awake, his eyes open, confused, hollowed by the edge of death's shadow.

Outside, stars clawed at the sky in their slow procession.

The stranger wrapped a cloak around the youth's shoulders, not his own, but a rough one folded near the bier, untouched by hands since the burial.

"Come," he said.

Miriam stepped forward, but he raised one finger. Not in warning. In reverence.

"He must walk tonight."

She stepped back, unsure, the braid falling loose behind her ear.

The stranger and the youth passed into the night.

Beyond the olive grove, past the threshold of Bethany, into a clearing where stone met moonlight. No rites followed them. No crowd. Only the hush of air that had witnessed too much.

They sat.

Neither spoke.

Then the youth wept.

"I saw nothing," he said. "Only forgetting."

The stranger placed his hand on the youth's chest.

"You were not meant to see," he whispered. "You were meant to be remembered."

"I was cold," said the youth. "And the cold was shaped like me."

"Yes."

"And it asked me a question."

"What question?"

"It asked, Why did you carry your longing inside your silence?"

The stranger did not answer.

Instead, he reached into the earth and drew a circle with his finger.

Twelve stones. Uneven. Ancient.

He placed a branch from the olive tree in the center.

Then he whispered again.

Not to the youth.

To the ache beneath him.

"Let this night become your breath."

They remained in the grove as night thickened.

The youth's shoulders curled inward, not from cold, but from the weight of questions he could not yet ask. The stranger offered no answers, only silence wide enough to hold grief and wonder alike. The olive branch in the center of the twelve stones began to shimmer with dew, though no mist had fallen.

"I remember," the youth said suddenly. "Not death. Not breath. But... voices."

The stranger tilted his head slightly.

"They whispered as if I'd been waiting since before I was born."

He looked at the stranger. "Did you call them?"

"No," came the reply. "They already knew your name."

The youth trembled. "I was not worthy."

The stranger touched his wrist, gently.

"Worth is dust," he said. "You are echo. You are vessel. And tonight, you begin to awaken the ache you were born to carry."

The wind shifted then, low and warm. The stones beneath them vibrated subtly, like memory tuning itself to new breath.

Then the stranger reached into the folds of his garment and drew forth something small.

A thread.

Dark, frayed, and pulsing faintly.

He placed it across the youth's palm.

"You were buried without story," he said. "This is the beginning."

The youth wrapped the thread around his finger. And as he did, his eyes changed, not with fire, not with light, but with depth. As though he were seeing the world through the eyes of someone yet to arrive.

"I am not who I was," he said.

The stranger stood.

"You never were."

Miriam waited in silence.

She had not moved from the threshold. Her braid now lay across her lap, the strands pulled loose by grief, touched only by wind.

When they returned, her eyes widened.

The youth walked steadily, the cloak around him woven now with light, as if moonlight had stitched itself into its fibers.

She rushed forward, paused, then touched his hand.

"It is warm," she whispered. "It is warm."

The stranger stepped aside.

She turned to him. "You did not raise him with power."

"No," he replied. "I raised him with memory."

"What memory?"

"The one that was braided into his bones before his first cry."

She lowered her gaze.

"I will feed him. Bathe him. Sing the chants."

"He will hear them differently now."

"And what of you?" she asked.

"I leave."

"Why?"

He said nothing.

Then he placed one hand upon the lintel of the house, where the wood was worn smooth. He touched a single groove, perhaps carved, perhaps natural and whispered into it.

Miriam did not hear the word. But the air shifted.

She bowed her head.

"You are not the one we were told to expect," she said.

"No," he answered. "I am the silence before expectation."

Then he walked into the night.

The youth did not speak much in the days that followed. His breath came easily, his body moved without pain, but something in him remained quiet, not withdrawn, not afraid, but listening.

Miriam sang while she baked, brushing oil across flatbread in patterns she used to trace on his brow as a child. He watched her hands, and with each gesture, felt something stir beneath the surface of remembering.

But it was not her voice that woke him.

It was the circle.

Each night, he returned alone to the clearing, to the twelve stones still resting where they had been placed, weathered now by dew and the trace of something ancient left in the soil. The olive branch had dried, curled into a spiral. He did not remove it.

He sat among the stones, letting silence pour over him like a river. And each night, he heard the whisper again.

Not from the stranger. From within.

You were braided into the ache.

At first, the phrase meant nothing. A thread of mystery without tension. But then came the dream.

He stood beside a fig tree that bled light from its fruit. A woman in shadow knelt beneath it, her braid unbound, her voice folded into ritual. She reached out and placed a thread in his palm, dark, trembling, marked with the sound of his own heartbeat.

"You will carry breath where breath has been forgotten," she said.

And he woke.

Tears lined his cheeks, but his chest did not shake. He was not weeping.

He was receiving.

A story, not his, not new, was braiding itself into him.

And though the stranger was gone, the youth felt him still, not behind, but beneath. Like roots remembering the shape of water.

He whispered, not to the stars, but to the spiral in the soil.

"I am not returned," he said.

"I am begun."

"He did not conquer. He did not announce. He knelt. And the stones wept as if memory had returned to earth. Even the sky paused. In that stillness, the world did not resume, it re-began."

Ezra ben Talmai, son of the gardener of Bethany, was ten when the veil thinned. For fifty years he told no one. Until one moonless night, beneath a lamp that flickered like breath, he spoke into the quiet. That whisper outlived him.

Chapter Twenty - Pilgrim of the Silent Kingdoms

In the esrin w-arba shnin of his breath, the boy walked not with time, but through it.

He passed through lands of breath and bell, territories untouched by empire, mapped only by silence strung like prayer flags across snow. In Benares, the air carried turmeric and longing. In Rajgir, monks bowed not to him, but to a presence sensed in the hush of his stillness. No name was asked. No miracle performed. Yet the fire in his eyes turned winter away.

He slept beneath Bodhi trees whose roots brushed memory and wandered into Himalayan passes where the wind whispered the Upanishads to him, not as scripture, but as song. It was here, among saffron-robed seekers and outcast saints, that he tasted teachings born not of decree but of breath, how compassion flows without hierarchy, and truth wears no garb but humility.

They called him Issa, the foreign one, who did not speak much but heard everything. When the caste bound refused him food, he gave a smile that softened stone. When asked about God, he pointed to the stars and said, "That which made them also gave you the eyes to see."

Through years that blurred like incense in motion, he learned not to preach, but to kneel beside suffering. To wait. To weep without shame. These were lessons not found in Torah scrolls, but in silence shared over cracked bowls of rice and barefoot journeys through unmarked paths.

One night, in a monastery draped in moonlight, he asked an elder, "What lies beyond this journey?"

The reply came as mist, "Not beyond, but within. The stars you seek now wait for you to notice their echo inside."

And with that, the boy, Issa, wanderer of kingdoms unmapped, turned toward the West, his heart filled not with doctrine, but with a language only compassion could speak.

Four and twenty winters had peeled their skins from the sky since the comet hung over a manger and the boy of sand and mystery breathed his first. Now, his stride was leaner, his silence more practiced, his gaze hollowed not by sorrow but by seeing too much of what others missed.

The sages of Nalanda called him the foreign petal, for he bloomed in their courtyards and drifted on before any root could hold him. He came not to study, they said, but to remember. And what he remembered was not from scroll or stone, but from the sound shadows make when spoken of with reverence.

A particular monk, known only as Gnyanaraksha, watched the boy in silence. His name meant "Protector of Knowing," but he had given up knowing long ago. He saw the wanderer sit by the river that bifurcated the monastery, and without ceremony, the monk sat beside him.

"Have you come from the deserts of the West?" he asked, voice wrapped in a breeze.

Issa did not answer.

"Then perhaps you have come from the place before birth," the monk said, nodding as though that explained everything.

That night, Gnyanaraksha led him to the chamber of bells, a place where initiates were taught to ring silence into the world. Here, Issa did not touch any of the hundred bronze bells. Instead, he traced the dust on their surface, leaving no mark. The monks whispered among themselves, "He listens for what the bells fear to speak."

For three lunar cycles, Issa remained. He said nothing of divinity. He argued not against doctrine. Yet when the young monks gathered to read the Lotus Sutra, he listened so deeply the syllables seemed to rest on his skin before entering the chamber of his thoughts.

When asked what he believed, he pointed to the river,

"It forgets, and it still flows."

They called this Issa's Sutra of Forgetting, and many monks left their stations to follow the river into obscurity, convinced they had learned the most difficult wisdom, how not to be remembered, yet change everything.

The pilgrim, he who bore no title, no staff, no lineage claimed aloud, walked the footpaths where snow dared not settle. The monks of the high monastery whispered of a cave that drank time, whose walls knew the breath of sages long returned to ash. They did not guide him there. They simply said, "It listens."

He ascended alone.

The air thinned. Language fled. Even memory bent.

Within the cave, there were no carvings. No altar. Just silence shaped like stone, and stone shaped like silence.

He sat cross legged, arms open, not in supplication, but invitation. The hush around him did not press inward, it bloomed outward. It was there, in that primordial dark, that he heard the flame without fire.

No vision. No apparition.

Only a vibration older than sound.

It said nothing.

And yet, its presence throbbed with a question he had carried since his twelfth winter, one that had lingered behind every gesture, every exile, every tear he refused to shed,

"Will you forget your name so the world may remember its breath?"

He did not answer.

But the wind behind his ribs shifted.

And in that moment, the cave blinked, a faint pulse passed through it, like the heartbeat of a dying star remembering its birth.

When he emerged, his eyes held the hue of dusk, not fatigue, not sorrow, but the color of things unseen.

She sat beneath the tree as if placed there by wind, her body small, her braid thick with ash and silver. Her name, if asked, would be lost. She did not offer it. Instead, she held a single fig in her palm, bleeding light along its skin. He approached, not for fruit, but for story.

"You have walked far," she said. "But the walking is never the longest part."

He nodded.

"I once touched the robe of the one who renounced kingdoms," she whispered. "Not because I believed, but because I saw how the soil bowed beneath his feet."

He knelt beside her. Not in worship. In listening.

"The robe was coarse," she said. "No embroidery. But it carried the scent of longing, like cinnamon braided with distance."

She placed the fig in his hand.

"There is no teaching," she said. "Only the memory of how to taste."

He bit into it.

And felt centuries dissolve across his tongue.

Issa's feet kissed the edge of the Zagros Mountains, where the night air spoke in sighs and the stones remembered stories no scribe had written. In a small village carved into ochre cliffs, a woman sang a lullaby to a dying fire. She saw him approach but did not pause her song. Its cadence braided into the wind, and the wanderer bowed, not to her, but to the syllables carried beyond her breath.

Inside her home, which smelled of smoke and saffron, she offered him water from a cracked clay cup. It tasted not of earth, but of forgetting, the kind that lets one sleep again after mourning.

"They say you've come from lands where truth rides in on thunder," she said. "Here, it walks barefoot and wears no cloak."

Issa drank, and the silence between them became thick, like honey before harvest.

Later, in the ruins of Persepolis where moonlight strokes ancient pillars like lost lovers, he sat where kings once feasted and heard the dust recite its genealogy. Shadows of empire drifted by, asking nothing of him. He watched as moths circled broken carvings and though, "Even light is drawn to what cannot be rebuilt."

A child found him there, with eyes like almond bark and fingers that played a melody on broken flutes. She spoke in riddles she did not know were ancient, "What is softer than silence and heavier than memory?" He did not answer. She smiled as if he had. "That's right," she said, and gave him a reed.

With it, he carved no sound. He simply kept it close. A relic not of power, but presence.

Weeks turned like prayer wheels, and Issa entered the lands of sand and shadow, Petra, city of rose, where tombs slept upright. Traders passed him speaking tongues layered with salt and suspicion. He gave no name. And so, they gave him many.

One night, beneath an arch chiseled by stars, a man in blue robes asked him, "Do you come for prophecy?"

"I come," said Issa, "for the dust between prophecies."

The man smiled. "Then you've arrived too early or too late."

"That is the only time truth reveals itself."

They sat beside one another on stone warm from yesterday's heat. The man gave him a scroll he could not read, etched in a language that had died before language began. "It is not for your eyes," the man said. "It is for your silence."

Issa dreamt of a sea that breathed in reverse, waves rolling inward as if swallowing time. He awoke in Babylon's shadow, where reeds whispered to rivers and starlight arranged itself in equations that had no solution. There, under skies that bore the weight of ancient astrologers' doubts, he met a blind man named Othniel.

Othniel did not ask who he was. Instead, he traced the air around Issa's shoulders and said, "You carry weight not made of flesh."

Issa sat beside him for days, speaking nothing, until the blind man said, "You are ready."

"For what?"

"To leave."

"Leave what?"

"Even the question."

When Issa crossed into lands of olive and dust, the world did not notice. No procession met him. No prophecy bloomed. He passed through Galilee like wind through fig leaves, felt but unnamed.

In a field of barley swaying like whispered sorrow, he knelt beside an old woman gathering seeds. She told him of her son, a fisherman who no longer believed in tide or miracle. "He waits," she said, "but not for fish."

Issa touched her hand, not to heal, but to remember. And in that moment, she whispered a prayer without words, one she had forgotten until his silence reminded her how to speak.

And then came the cave again, not the one of bells, but a hollow carved into the flesh of dusk itself. It had no entrance. No exit. Only presence.

Issa entered, not with feet but with surrender.

Inside, the silence was louder than thought, older than creation's first echo. He did not kneel. He did not speak. He dissolved, not into nothing, but into the fabric of what forgets and still remembers.

A question came, not as voice, not even as vibration. It came as pause. As the moment before the fig is picked. As the breath before love becomes word.

It asked, "Will you allow mystery to pass through you without grasping it, and still call it truth?"

He did not answer.

He simply became.

He did not enter the village as a flame, but as a soft remainder of fire. The kind that lingers in stones long after the blaze has passed, warming without warning. The river, thin with summer, whispered as he walked. His feet stirred no dust. His presence, a hush over barley fields.

Children paused in their games, eyes following him not with curiosity, but recognition, though none could name what was known. They later drew spirals in the dirt where he'd passed, as if remembering something that hadn't yet happened.

An old woman, deaf to everything but starlight, heard Issa's silence and hummed a melody long buried beneath years. "He walks like absence wearing form," she said to no one, and someone wept at the truth of it.

One evening, a shepherd, dreaming beside his flock, spoke aloud in sleep, A widening ripple, sent by God to erase no one, but to soften the edge of forgetting. At dawn, he didn't recall the dream, but he did find a lamb born with eyes like dusk, deep, tender, and watching.

The village's songs changed. Not their words, nor their notes, but the breath between them. As if sung not to be heard, but to be remembered by the earth.

The morning was pale with mist, and the village still slept. Issa sat beneath a sycamore worn smooth by wind, its roots curled like listening hands. A young girl approached, hesitant. Her voice barely reached him.

"Why do you never speak?"

Issa opened his eyes. They held the weight of unspoken centuries.

He did not smile. He simply said, "Speech is the shadow of listening. And listening is the doorway to remembering who you were before you were named."

The child blinked, unsure whether she'd heard words or wind.

She ran home and told her mother, who told no one.

But that night, she dreamt of stars that whispered her own name back to her, not the one given at birth, but the one she'd nearly forgotten.

This single thread of sound rippled outward, not as a sermon, not as myth, but as a change in the way birds paused before flight. In the way villagers began to breathe before they answered each other. In the way grief began to hum in harmony with hope.

That is how it began.

Not with proclamation, but with breath made visible.

Issa was last seen walking toward the hills, not the storied ones of prophecy, but the quiet slopes that held no name and needed none. A child said she saw him touch a thornbush and whisper into its bloom. The next day, it flowered early.

Others say he left at dusk, the sky inked with swallows. A single footprint remained in river silt, vanishing with the next breeze.

But those who never met him began to change.

A potter stopped glazing his bowls and let them remain raw, unsealed, claiming that truth was more beautiful without finish.

A father who had buried a son unearthed the grave, not in madness, but to plant fig trees around it. He said, "Let breath live beside remembering."

A woman who'd stopped singing found herself humming while grinding grain. Not for joy. For balance.

And in the monastery of bells, one bronze bell rang of its own accord, though no hand moved. The monks gathered, hearts aching with wonder. One whispered, "He listens still."

Years passed.

Issa's name was not carved. His teachings were not penned.

But somewhere beneath the weight of tradition and the tremble of myth, a small thread remained dark, frayed, pulsing faintly.

Not tied to doctrine.

But woven through ache.

Beneath the fig tree, its limbs cradling starlight and the slow breath of dusk, the boy lingered. A single leaf touched his palm, tender veined, pulsing like a truth remembered. All around him, the world did not speak, yet it listened, river stones holding stories in silence, wind curled like a guardian around the hollow of his chest. He turned toward the wilderness, and in that gaze was no longing, no fear, only the knowing that the sky would not answer, but might reveal. The ground beneath him felt older now, as if it had once been walked by light itself, and the air shimmered with the memory of prayer, not in words, but in presence.

Chapter Twenty-one - He Who Stands Beneath the Quiet

He rises as he has each morning since the turning of his twenty-fifth year, not as ritual but as recognition, that the years have begun to etch meaning rather than merely pass. The fire still sleeps. The sky stirs gently. And he, no longer boy, not yet elder, kneels within the fragile quiet of becoming.

At twenty five, the ache in his bones carries memory, not exhaustion. His hands no longer grasp for answers, they receive silence as scripture. The prayer he knows now is not the fervent asking of adolescence, nor the certainty of scribes. It is breath drawn from the deep well of solitude, shaped by days wandered and questions unanswered.

He walks, and the land remembers him. The fig branches he had climbed at thirteen now cradle him in shade. The olive groves, where he once hid in the games of youth, whisper now of patience. At twenty five, he does not pray to be spared, or chosen, or seen. He prays to be hollowed, made vast enough for mystery.

The caves receive him differently now. At twenty five, he reads the fractures in the stone not as wounds, but as windows. He is a man standing at the edge of inheritance, not of land or name, but of vision. His brow, kissed by morning light, carries no crown, only sweat and dust, the coronation of the waiting.

And beneath the olive tree, he listens for the divine not in thunder but in the murmurs of bark and bird. He bows, not to offer, only to be unmade and remade, again and again. The prayer is in his limbs, his silence, his age. Twenty-five, where solitude does not frighten, and the sacred arrives slowly.

At twenty five, his prayer no longer sought to touch the divine, it allowed the divine to touch him, quietly, without arrival. As the sun climbed its first hour, washing the stone walls in pale gold, he sat where the fig trees stitched shadows into the soil, unmoving, as though his stillness encouraged time to linger.

No incense marked this invocation; no chanting rose to pierce the sky. His prayer moved beneath the skin, within breath and muscle, through memory and doubt, until his body became a vessel for what he could neither name nor command. He breathed, not to summon light, but to let it enter without permission.

In silence, he felt the years folded behind him, the wildness of childhood, the ache of early longing, the way questions once bloomed and died before reaching his lips. At twenty five, he did not ask anymore. He watched. He remembered. He waited.

The wind passed across the hills as if brushing pages of a hidden scroll. His fingers followed it through the air, tracing letters unseen, symbols that came not from ink but from time's hush. He knew the language of stones, of tears dried into grain, of voices abandoned in cave dust. These became his syllables. And he prayed not for clarity, but to remain open to mystery.

The prayer now moved through the valley where goats wandered, and grass bent without noise. He stood, his shadow long against the hillside, and as he walked, each step harmonized with rhythms older than birth. A shepherd watched from afar, unknowing, yet sensing that something holy passed near, not in form, but in stillness.

At twenty-five, his skin carried the sun not as burn but as belonging. His hair caught the wind like forgotten banners of longing. He reached the place where the old prophet once buried visions in jars, sealed with wax and hope. He sat among the forgotten, and in doing so, found the sacred.

His prayer gathered heat, not as fire, but as life within fire, the urge of stars to expand, the silence between quarks. It stretched through him like the beginnings of dawn behind mountains not yet touched by light. He was not waiting for revelation. He was becoming its echo.

The river called. Not with sound, but with gravity. He moved toward it slowly, not to cleanse, nor to cross, but to kneel beside its body, allowing the waters to whisper as breath does against sleeping skin. His fingers entered the current and let go of time.

He remembered being five, feeling eternity press into his ribs like the touch of a spirit without name. Now, at twenty five, he let that same spirit move through him, without resistance, without form. The divine did not hover above, it pulsed within.

At this age, prayer became his quiet rebellion against all things spoken too loud. Against answers packaged and truths polished. He walked the ridge at dusk and did not seek miracle, only presence. The sky unfolded, not as canvas, but as mirror and he saw in its vastness the shape of his own longing.

He returns from the river not cleansed but composed, his steps tracing the memory of where water met skin and left its mark without sound. At twenty five, his body is no longer searching for ritual, it has become the ritual. The ground beneath him does not wait to be sanctified. It receives him as flame receives wick, as dusk receives color.

The place he chooses to kneel is without ornament. No temple calls him. No altar beckons. Instead, he finds the grove where fig leaves curl in quiet lament, and the soil is dark with the knowing of roots. He bows, not with flourish, but with the weight of one who has forgotten the difference between prayer and breathing.

He lowers himself slowly, deliberately, his spine folding like parchment touched by centuries of wind. At twenty five, he understands that the divine does not ask for speed. It waits behind stillness, watching how the soul unfurls when no one sees.

His breath becomes the first stanza, drawn in through the nose as though he is inhaling the memory of stars not yet named. He holds it, not to control, but to feel the shape of longing. Then releases, not to dismiss, but to offer. Each breath is liturgy. Each pause, a psalm.

He does not speak, though words spiral within him like incense undone by wind. They are words of earlier years, fragments of scrolls, murmurs from prophets whose hands once trembled beneath visions. He lets them rise, then fall. His prayer is not in their utterance but in their surrender.

The grove darkens slightly. The sun moves, barely noticeable. And in this slow passage of light, he finds what language cannot offer, a sense that he is being watched, not from above, but from within. The prayer rises like warmth in his chest, not sharp, but aching, like something ancient remembering itself.

He opens his eyes not to end the prayer, but to allow it to shift. A goat passes in the distance, a bird cuts the sky, and each movement becomes part of the invocation. At twenty five, he no longer separates sacred from simple. The reed swaying beside him is a verse. The insect crawling across his wrist is an Amen.

He stands, slowly, letting his limbs remember that flesh itself can worship, not by gestures taught, but by presence maintained. He walks now, not to arrive, but to extend the prayer into motion. His feet press against the earth with reverence, heel then toe, each step a syllable in the unfolding mystery.

He finds the hillside where light lingers longest before twilight, and there he sits again, spine tall, palms open beside him. No relics in hand. No sacred garment. Only twenty five years of listening, and the sound of wind through olive branches.

The prayer continues, not from will, but from willingness. Not from scripture, but from silence. He understands now, the divine does not dwell in thunder, nor require fire to descend. It comes softly, when a man no longer asks to be filled but chooses to be empty. Emptied of striving. Emptied of needing. Emptied of anything but awe.

And as stars begin their ascent, quietly blinking into place as if summoned by breath, he remains. Still, quiet, a man not praying to be answered, but to remain open. The night envelopes him. And somewhere in that darkness, the sacred enters, not as voice, but as presence too vast to speak.

The moon passed overhead like a silent psalm. He had grown accustomed to its pale visitation, the way it strained against the black, never quite triumphant, yet always bearing witness.

He closed his eyes.

A reed of breath uncoiled from his chest. Not the breath of speech, not even of naming, but the breath that precedes all creation. It moved through him like wind through wheat, an ancient rhythm awakening. Beneath his ribs, the soil of memory quivered. In its quiet furrows bloomed the scent of cedar, river silt, and the burning hush of stars.

He felt the veil again. Not torn. Not rent. But thinned, as though the lattice between all things had momentarily flickered. Through it poured whispers, not of language, but of longing.

And he prayed, not upward, not outward, but inward and through. The mountains within him lifted their heads, and the rivers turned.

There, in the hollow hour, when the world no longer pretended to be solid, he became luminous. Not with light, but with weightlessness. His name, spoken once, echoed into the folds of everything. A name not uttered by lips, but by being.

He did not need to understand.

He simply entered.

The first signs came not as blaze, but as breath, the kind of light that touches the earth so softly it seems to ask permission. He felt it before he saw it, the shift in silence, the way darkness loosened its hold on the edges of things. His limbs stirred as if beckoned by gravity reimagined, his spine rising without thought, just as reeds straighten when dawn arrives.

At twenty-five, he had learned not to rush the light. Prayer is made complete not by climax, but by stillness sustained. He watched the sky draw color like ink into vellum, slow as remembering. Each hue a verse. Each cloud a line crossing time.

He moved through the grove again fig leaves trembling like pages turned by wind and returned to the clearing where soil bore the imprint of last night's kneeling. The air was cold still, but not severe. It felt honest. Like the breath of one who speaks only when truth is ready.

He knelt again, not to begin, but to honor the thread. The prayer had slept alongside him. Now it rose.

His breath was gentler now, wrapped in gratitude shaped without word. He did not give thanks. He embodied it. The wind touched his brow and found it willing.

The divine within him no longer stirred with fire but with light, slow light, low light, the kind that gathers without announcement. At twenty-five, he did not pray for answers. He allowed himself to become the question.

He lifted his hands, not high, but forward, palms open like the unfurling petals of a bloom whose roots drink mystery. He touched nothing, yet felt held. No response came, but presence deepened, braided into breath and bone.

The prayer spread; into muscle, into morning, into memory. It walked beside him as he stood. It moved with him as he gathered water in a shallow bowl. It remained as he sipped. It listened as he breathed. It did not demand. It did not depart.

And when the sun finally crowned the ridge, he stood facing it, not as worshipper, but as echo. The light met his skin and did not burn. It recognized him. And in that recognition, the prayer, his prayer, the prayer of twenty-five years searching and surrendering, did not end. It flowed on. Quiet. Cosmic. Unbreakable.

He stood as if called, not by voice, but by gravity reimagined. The grove behind him breathed the silence of answered questions, and the wind pulled gently at his garments like pages wanting to be read again. At twenty-five, he had become the still point, the nexus where time forgets to divide itself.

Light unfurled in layers, not just across the ridge but across his being, each ray a testament to what had passed through him, sorrow and stars, hunger and holiness, the ache of knowing without proof, the joy of surrender without promise.

The world did not change around him.

He changed within it.

Prayer had undone him.

Not erased.

Revealed.

The soil beneath his feet no longer held him, it embraced him. The sky above did not simply watch, it remembered him. And every breath from here forward would carry a signature written in silence, traced in the dialect of the divine, etched into the soft architecture of listening.

His spine rose tall, not in pride, but in reverence. His eyes, open, did not seek, they bore witness. The sacred did not descend. It had always been rising. And now, within him, it stood.

He walked forward, into the light, into the breath, into the world that remained unchanged yet entirely new.

And behind him, the grove whispered the name no mouth shall speak, the name once buried in starlight and resurrected in silence, the name not given, but become.

Chapter Twenty-two - The Lamentation and the Longing

He knelt where the wind was ancient. Not the wind that scraped the sand with fury, but the kind that remembered creation, the kind that carried whispers buried beneath centuries of stars. This was not a temple, not a gathering place, not even a shelter from the cold. It was the inward spiral of stillness, a space between pulses where breath became prayer before it touched the lips.

Around him, the stones listened. They had no tongue, no eyes, no memory bound to flesh. Yet they remembered differently. They remembered footsteps long gone. They remembered those who spoke not for the sake of answers, but for the sake of release. They remembered laments that bore no audience, save for the silence itself.

He bowed low, forehead grazing stone, and his breath spread thin beneath him. The soul within him had wandered across years, had touched both hunger and healing, had spoken in languages lost to flame and flood. Now, at this threshold between youth and fullness, sorrow gathered in his marrow. Not a sorrow of self, but of the countless faces flickering in his mind, each one cloaked in longing that never fully bloomed.

The breath he gave was not just his own. It bore the weight of mothers who buried sons without name, of elders whose eyes grew blind waiting for the dawn that never kissed their gates.

Each inhalation was a rustle in the void, and every exhalation a ghost pulled from the marrow.

"Let the earth speak," he whispered, not aloud, not to be heard by another, but into the belly of silence itself.

The wind answered in no tongue he knew, but in rhythm. Soft pulses. A beat, then stillness. A beat, then stillness. He followed it into the hollow beneath ribs and bone, and there, the lament unfurled.

O Voice who made the fig to blossom in drought,

why do you tarry when the child thirsts for fire and mercy?

Was the world shaped to hear itself suffer,

or did the song twist upon the string when the stars were young?

His words were salted. Not with tears alone, but with time. Dialect bled through them, not crafted, not polished. It came from the mud between fields, from the whisper of old men beside cracked wells.

"Yah sh'lama," he murmured, the Aramaic bleeding through lips like wine from clay cups. "Lama takhlan di b'rahma, w'la chaze." Peace be with me, why do You devour with mercy, yet remain unseen.

He was not asking for the veil to be torn. Only for it to breathe.

Around him, insects moved like sacred scribes, writing nothing, everything, on the sand. The firelight in the sky began its descent, amber and violet folding into the mountains like a prayer remembered at dusk.

He sat, back against the stone, and let his voice fall again.

My bones recall a garden untouched,

where rivers were not cruel and light did not choose who it kissed.

Tell me, O Vastness,

do You mourn with me, or have You forgotten how to cry?

The voice came not as thunder, nor whisper. It came as ache. As the trembling under the skin when no one else is near. As the hush that lingers after truth is spoken but not believed.

He did not lift his eyes. The sky no longer promised revelations. Instead, he listened to the way dusk folded over the hills like mourning cloth, how the shadows crept not in fear, but in wearied reverence. Beneath his skin, a tremble moved, quiet as the breath before a newborn's first cry.

Words came like smoke rising from cracked olivewood.

"The stars do not pity," he said, not to anyone, yet not to himself. "They spin, they burn, they die silent deaths." His tongue curled around dust-cloaked syllables, speech learned not from books but from the belly of exile. "And still, I envy them. For they do not remember."

Memory, he tasted it like bitter resin. It had no mercy, no threshold of forgetting. It clung to him like fire to dry reeds, and every footstep he'd taken stirred ghosts that asked for nothing but to be heard once more.

He prayed, not with certainty, not with boldness, but with cracked voice and curled fingers.

Oh, You who remain unnamed,

whose breath touches fig leaf and raven alike,

do You feel the ache of those who call to You with no reply?

Do You sit in silence because words are too small for love?

A child once cried beside him, years ago, alone in the borderlands. No mother came. No songs were sung. Only wind. Only him. He remembered holding the child's hand until the sun gave itself back to the mountain.

"Tamir yah." Hidden One. He spoke again, "Ma hazit, ma hazit…" What did You see, what did You see…

His voice faltered.

Each sentence fell like a stone into a well, never reaching water, only echo.

He pressed his palm to the earth, where the soil was bruised with roots and stone, and whispered again—not with hope, but with reverence for grief that had not yet spoken its last.

The voice within him curled like incense smoke, rising without flame.

You are the One who walks with light and does not burn,

the One whose gaze touched the serpent, the fig, the frost of morning,

and did not flinch.

Why then do You shroud Yourself from those who ask without armor?

There was no reply, only the hush between wind gusts. Yet that hush had form. It moved as memory moves—not with footsteps, but with breath.

He turned his face toward the edge of the hills, where old fig trees knelt toward sky like elders at prayer. Their branches were gnarled, hollow in places, trembling with the age of worlds. From them he heard a whisper, not with ears, but with soul.

"Nuach. Sce'anan. Bo b'or" Rest. Be still. Enter the light.

It was no command. No comfort, even. It was a murmur. Like the last voice of a dream before waking—a dialect older than speech. Aramaic braided with something beyond time.

He held it. Not the meaning, but the feeling. The ache that light could sometimes be a silence too deep for words.

Years earlier he had walked through villages forgotten by maps. Faces turned from him, not in hate, but in hunger for what he could not give. He had given bread, given touch, given stories that wrapped around the wounded like balm. Yet still, their eyes asked more. Asked for revelation. Asked for the tearing of veils.

He could not tear the veil. Only dwell beneath it.

So now he prayed again. Not with clarity, but with lament.

O Vastness whose pulse is within rain and ruin,

do You remember the face of those who cry without sound?

Do You bind together the broken reeds,

or do You leave them, like me, scattered beneath Your stars?

He felt the weight of longing then, not just his own, but of every soul that ever gazed upward and found no answer. It was a cosmic ache. A pain shaped not by cruelty, but by distance. A love too deep to touch, too wide to hold.

And in that ache, he did not turn away.

He offered his voice one more time. Not to change the silence, but to join it.

Yakh tamun...

you know the sorrow of unspoken names.

You know the tremble of hands that reach without hope.

And still, you remain.

The silence did not respond in words. It moved more subtly, like the way shadows shift when no one's watching, or how the body learns to grieve before the mind understands it.

He stood slowly, dust trailing from his robe like old memory. His feet found the rhythm of the ground again, a sacred hum beneath the surface. In the west, clouds gathered, not for rain, but as witness. They pulsed with orange, with bruised lilac, with the hush of twilight that had never once betrayed him.

He spoke again.

You, who do not count the tears but keep their weight,

You who inhabit the pause between questions,

are You the ache in the child who reaches for bread,

or the bread that chooses not to fall?

195

He felt the words leave him like warmth from a dying fire. They did not return, nor did they need to. Prayer, he knew, was not dialogue. It was offering. Lamentation was not request. It was witness.

The stones beneath him warmed with remembered sun. He traced a circle with his fingers, dust swirling within the gesture. A ritual older than text, older than law. A prayer etched in motion, not in doctrine.

From within, the longing stirred again, not toward miracles, but toward presence. The presence that required nothing except willingness to remain.

He looked toward the east, where the night had begun to sing.

Its song was voiceless, yet layered, crickets, faint winds, distant waterfalls whispering their descent through the veins of rock. Nature did not grieve. It bore sorrow and joy in equal breath.

And he whispered,

> I have walked with hunger, not for food,
>
> but for the voice You spoke into fig tree and flame.
>
> I have heard stories of angels and thunder,
>
> but I do not seek them.

I seek only the ache that binds You to me,

the ache that does not ask to be healed.

His eyes closed.

The prayer was not finished. It would never be. But something within it had begun to settle. Not as answer, but as breath that does not flee.

He waited there beneath the constellation of the weaver, whose threads stretched across the firmament. And in that waiting, he gave silence the last word.

The silence did not respond in words. It moved more subtly—like the way shadows shift when no one's watching, or how the body learns to grieve before the mind understands it.

He stood slowly, dust trailing from his robe like old memory. His feet found the rhythm of the ground again, a sacred hum beneath the surface. In the west, clouds gathered, not for rain, but as witness. They pulsed with orange, with bruised lilac, with the hush of twilight that had never once betrayed him.

The stars had gathered now, not to proclaim, but to listen.

Their light did not instruct. It hovered. Dimmed. Returned. Like breath from an unseen body. In their quiet constellation, he found no map, only the same question rising as mist from the ribs,

What does mercy sound like when no voice speaks it?

He lay upon the earth, arms open, palms turned skyward. Beneath him, the soil trembled, not with tremor, but with memory. It had swallowed rain and fire. It had born witness to footprints that vanished without trace. Now it held him, not as prophet, not as stranger, but as dust returned to its echo.

Above, the night deepened. A meteor trailed across the belly of Orion, dissolving like a last kiss. The air thinned with holiness.

In the cave behind him, shadows nested, old and unafraid. From within their hush came one final whisper,

"Yoshev baShamayim." He dwells in the heavens.

But he did not seek the heavens.

He sought the place where heavens weep.

He rose, not abruptly, but as flame rises from ember. Eyes open, gaze soft, he turned once more toward the fig tree bent in prayer. Its branches held the memory of rain. Its roots drank silence like wine.

And then he spoke, not to summon, not to teach, not to finish—

But to become.

You who do not answer,

You who made absence holy,

I leave my voice with You.

Not that You may speak,

but that You may remember.

The final word was not his. It belonged to wind.

And in the wind, the longing remained.

Chapter Twenty-three - Beneath the Waters That Do Not Speak

He had seen twenty-six winters, though he no longer counted seasons by snow or bloom. The age settled into him not as number, but as a kind of shadow that walked beside the breath. It spoke without sound, taught without tongue. It marked him with questions that had no answers and longings that did not dissolve.

He awoke before the sky bruised itself with morning. The cave behind him still carried the scent of fireless nights. Beneath his feet, the stones were colder than memory. He stepped slowly, tracing the shape of unseen prayers with each movement. Not to arrive. But to remain.

No one had followed him into this wilderness. No one had asked for his return. And still, he walked.

He had become the echo of questions left unanswered, the pulse of wind that remembered voices too sacred to speak aloud. No lament rose from him now. Only a quiet seeking. And that seeking was older than fire.

His feet found their way to the stream that did not glitter. It moved without music, without the boast of light. Its waters slid like memory across stone, cool and dark and without reflection. This was not the river that carved valleys. It was the one that whispered to the unseen, carrying sorrows in its current and never returning them.

He knelt at its edge, palms grazing the soil as if asking permission.

The wind paused.

It was not obedience. It was reverence.

He lowered his face and did not ask for cleansing. Only to be held.

> You who knew me before I knew longing,
>
> who watched my voice form beneath ribs,
>
> do You wait at the river's end,
>
> or are You the water that refuses to speak?

The silence did not tremble.

He listened to the language of water that echoed without vowels. It did not rhyme. It did not soothe. But it carried the ache of a thousand voices, some unborn, some forgotten, some waiting still beneath the veil.

He dipped his fingers into the stream, slow and deliberate, as if touching a story too sacred to read aloud.

The cold did not hurt. It reminded.

Behind him, the cave remained. Its breath no longer reached him. He had moved beyond its threshold now—not in distance, but in becoming. The wilderness did not need to surround him anymore. It had folded into him.

A voice rose, but it was not sound.

It was the movement of fireflies beneath the fig tree's roots, the bend of mountains under starfall, the way silence gazed back when unafraid.

He sat upon a flat stone, shoulders bowed, eyes half-lidded.

Not asleep. Not awake.

Somewhere in between.

There was a story he carried, one without beginning, without conclusion. It came from dreams not dreamt, words not yet born. It came in fragments.

A woman who sang to vines but could not hear her own song.

A man who built houses no one entered.

A child who buried feathers beneath stones, hoping wings would rise.

Each fragment stirred inside him, not as memory, but as echo.

He placed his hand to his chest. The pulse was steady.

And he whispered,

O You who do not cure the ache,

but give it shape,

make of me not a mouth, but a listening.

Make of me not light, but the dusk before it.

Make of me not flame,

but the warmth left in its absence.

The stream continued its slow sermon.

No ripples. No rise.

Yet it moved with certainty.

He did not speak again for a long while. The body remained still, but within him, galaxies turned. They did not blaze. They unfolded.

They whispered the language of quiet stars.

He began to hum—not with melody, but with breath. It matched the stream, matched the wind, matched the murmur of fig trees folding themselves toward sky. The hum was not for performance. It was for remembering.

And in that remembering, another voice stirred.

Not divine. Not foreign.

It was the voice of childhood, aged and barefoot, sitting beneath moonlight and whispering riddles to beetles.

The voice said, "Walk gently. Not because the path is sacred, but because you are."

He rose again, slowly.

The stream was behind him.

It had never asked for worship.

Only witness.

He turned toward the east, where clouds had begun to gather like scripture. Their shape did not resemble animals or angels. They were neither revelation nor omen.

They were simply present.

Like him.

He walked until the fig tree reappeared, its branches still bowed, its leaves still whispering.

He sat beneath it and leaned into the soil.

Again, he offered no prayer.

Only presence.

Only the shape of longing, unspoken and vast.

And the wind resumed its breath.

Chapter Twenty-four - A Letter Never Sent

He found the tree again, not the fig tree, but another. This one leaned with a crooked grace, as if time had folded it sideways but spared its breath. Beneath its arching limbs, the ground was softer, less certain. The roots did not hold tightly to the earth, they hovered, exposed, like truths too raw to bury.

He knelt there. Twenty seven winters had passed him, though this season held no snow. The air moved with a stillness that did not belong to wind, but to memory.

He lifted a shard of bark, flat and mottled like old skin. He had no ink. No parchment. No seal to close. But he had words, unwritten, unbeckoned, drifting just beneath his ribs.

With the tip of his finger, he began to inscribe on the bark, not for others to read, but for silence to hold,

Mother, I have forgotten the sound of your footsteps, but not the way they

softened when you neared me.

The bread you made, its warmth did not last, but its grace did.

I never learned to say goodbye. Only to leave gently.

He paused. The bark pulsed with breathless waiting. The tree did not stir but listened.

He wrote again,

To the man whose shadow I wore as a child, I do not know your name.

Only your absence, and its shape. I sometimes hum without knowing why.

Maybe your voice was a melody too brief to remember.

The wind brushed the leaves. Not in interruption, but in assent.

To the child I will never hold, if you live only in my longing,

then let that longing be kind to you. Do not become a question.

Become a murmur that never demands reply.

His hand trembled, not from cold, but from the ache of unfinished words.

And then,

O You who do not reside in temples,

but in breath drawn beneath sorrow,

I do not write to summon You.

I write to remain near when my voice falters.

You need no letter.

But I needed to write one.

He placed the bark beneath the tree's root, pressed it into the earth with his palm.

The ground did not take it quickly. It held it a moment longer, like a hand reluctant to let go.

He rose, the silence folding around him like a cloak.

The letter was never meant to be delivered.

Only whispered to the soil.

Only known by the wind.

The bark remained beneath the root, neither forgotten nor reclaimed. It lay between soil and sky, a prayer untranslated, waiting to dissolve.

He did not turn from the tree. Not yet.

He sat once more, and memory did not rise as vision or voice, but as pulse, a kind of unseen scroll unrolling within the chest.

From deep within that silence, a sentence pressed against him.

The kingdom is within and without,

yet it cannot be sought with eyes open only to flame.

He had not read that line. He had breathed it, once, long ago, when the sky fractured with light that did not consume. It echoed in his ribs like a seed forming fruit.

A figure appeared, not of flesh, nor of light, but of ache. It did not speak. It shimmered. Its presence held both comfort and undoing.

In its silence, he heard,

I am the mind of those who dwell in wonder,

I am the speaking of those who are not believed.

I am the forgotten and the remembered.

I do not dwell in temples built of certainty.

He did not bow. He listened.

The figure drifted across him like wind through fig leaves. And he recalled a word never spoken aloud.

Barbelo.

The thought trembled. Not as name, but as breath that had never left the lungs. The First Thought. The Womb of the Unbegotten. She whose silence bore echo.

She remained only as sensation and in that presence, he felt the ache of many paths.

The child who once reached toward sky and asked, "Which sun is mine?"

The elder who stitched clay vessels in silence, waiting for rain that had not yet dreamed of falling.

The voice that spoke riddles in the desert and vanished before they were answered.

And he remembered another line, not from men, not from law, but from wind.

> Whoever drinks from the spring that is Me will return, not to where they were,
>
> but to where they have always been.

He rose gently. Not to leave the tree, but to continue its memory.

On the ground, he traced a circle, not with calculation, but with reverence. Within the circle he wrote a single word, a breath of longing.

Shalem.

Wholeness. Not as completion, but as return.

The earth held the word.

He did not speak again.

The soil beneath him still held the bark as if considering it, not to judge, not to bury, but to hold a breath before exhaling. It seemed the world had learned to pause. Not from fear. But from reverence.

Around him, light sifted through the branches in specks that moved like old alphabets. These were not letters to be read. They were to be remembered. A script that belonged to the heart before language was born.

And as he watched them flicker, he felt a presence beside him.

It was not a figure. Not a form. It was the echo of a thought too vast for syllables. It came with the scent of desert rain and the breath of ancient dawn.

In its presence, he recalled the utterance buried in the scrolls once hidden in valleys.

That which you seek is within you.

The veil is drawn not by hands, but by forgetting.

He placed his hand to the earth once more, tracing a spiral slowly.

It was not ritual.

It was remembering.

He did not speak. He did not pray.

He listened.

And within the hush, another memory rose, not from the world, but from the wound beneath the world.

The elder who once painted stars onto clay, saying, "These are not for heaven. These are so my hands remember."

The child who spoke to stones and waited for their reply, certain that the wind translated their voices.

The one who wandered barefoot through salt lakes, whispering to the light," You forgot me. But I never forgot you."

He breathed them all in.

Not to know them.

But to carry them.

Within this breath, he recalled a phrase once spoken in a dream, "The light speaks softly, lest it shatter the ears of those still grieving."

He stood slowly, brushing dust from his knees, though it seemed the dust clung out of longing. Beneath his feet, the earth pulsed.

Not loudly. But as a sigh.

The fig tree before him leaned deeper, as if to speak. Yet no voice rose.

And still, he understood.

He began to walk. Not toward, not away. But through.

The grove opened gently, like pages of a scroll parting not to be read, but to be held.

Ahead, a woman knelt by the river's bend.

Her robes were woven from dusk, not of thread, but of stillness. Her face held no age, no youth. She was neither invitation nor warning.

She was presence.

She did not look up but spoke. Her voice was less word than wind, "You carry sorrow as one who has met silence and not fled. You carry silence as one who has listened deeply and not claimed."

He did not answer.

And she said, "There is a place within the ache where light curls itself inward. Not to hide. But to rest. "

He knelt beside her.

Not to learn.

But to remember.

And in the space between them, something shimmered.

Not revelation.

But return.

She placed a stone into his palm, a smooth fragment etched with circles, one inside another. It warmed as if touched by fire, though no flame was near.

He understood.

It was not a token.

It was a question.

And so, he closed his fingers around it. And did not speak.

The river moved beside them, not with rhythm, but with remembrance. The water here did not reflect. It absorbed.

And as they sat, twilight began its descent, gentle and without warning.

The woman rose first, offering no farewell. She stepped into the grove, and with each step, the leaves bent slightly toward her, as if bowing to breath.

He remained.

He looked at the stone in his hand.

Then turned his eyes to the sky.

It did not blaze.

It waited.

And in that waiting, he offered a final whisper.

O One who trembles within stillness,

do not speak if the word would undo the hush.

Do not answer if the answer would silence the ache.

Remain with me as echo,

not as conclusion.

The wind stirred again.

It did not reply.

It remembered.

Twilight did not fall, it glided.

It moved like a veil drawn across the eyes not to dim vision, but to tender it. The stones grew quieter beneath his steps, their edges softened by the hush that followed the wind. He walked from the fig grove slowly, carrying no bark, no vessel, only the memory of a letter never sent and a voice that had not replied, yet remained.

The hills folded inward, shaped not by time, but by grief that once chose gentleness. He passed a cluster of reeds trembling without music. Their motion was not dance; it was ritual. They seemed to bow toward him without knowing why.

He turned once to glimpse the tree again. It did not call. It did not grieve. It watched—the way elders watch those who no longer need words.

Further on, the air changed. Thinner now. It held the scent of stone warmed during day but cooling into story. He knelt and placed his hand upon one, flat and fissured, its cracks reminding him of scripture not torn, but touched too often.

He whispered,

<blockquote>
You who dwell within forgetting,

You who carve absence into presence,

let me walk not in certainty,

but in awe.
</blockquote>

The sky darkened. A single star emerged, unrushed, almost reluctant. It did not shine. It hovered. It waited.

He walked again.

217

Each step now bore resemblance to his own heartbeat, rhythmic, quiet, expectant. The world did not open to him. It folded more tightly, like wings closing around something unseen.

He approached a path lined with ash trees.

Their bark peeled slowly in curled fragments, each strip a verse the wind read without voice. And in their reach, he remembered a passage once dreamt,

> If you do not bring forth what is within you,
>
> what you do not bring forth will destroy you.

The words did not frighten him. They confirmed something he already knew.

He reached the end of the grove and stood before a small rise, not a mountain, not even a hill, but a place that seemed to lean upward without ambition.

He climbed it.

Not for height, but for solitude.

At its crest, the wind rose once more, this time full bodied. It carried with it the scent of fig sap and dewless rain. He stood with his arms open, not wide, but sufficient.

A voice stirred in the wind, not foreign, not his own.

Let your longing become your teacher.

Let your silence become your mirror.

Let your forgetting become remembrance.

He breathed it in.

No fire appeared.

No angel descended.

No veil tore.

And still, it was enough.

He sat once more. Eyes open. Hands resting on his knees. The stone beneath him hummed with old warmth.

The star above flickered again, not in brilliance, but in rhythm.

It matched his pulse.

And the twilight whispered,

You are not waiting.

You are becoming.

The wind began to hush as if the dusk had whispered enough.

He remained seated upon the crest of the low rise, the stone beneath him now cool, cradling rather than bearing. The sky above had thickened, not with storm or shadow, but with the stillness that arrives when the world exhales.

The solitary star, which had lingered above like a witness without judgment, pulsed once more.

And then, it dimmed.

It did not vanish in haste.

It dissolved.

Folded inward.

As if drawn back into the breath that first uttered it.

He did not react. His gaze did not change. He watched with reverence, not for the star's brilliance, but for its departure.

You, whose light taught me not to seek,

but to listen,

go now,

not because your shining is done,

but because your whisper has been heard.

He placed the stone, the gift from the woman, upon the ground beside him. It did not roll. It rested in place, content with stillness.

He traced a spiral around it, then a circle. Not for protection, not for marking. But for remembrance.

Below, the valley hummed with the sleep of trees. No fires burned. No voices rose. The land itself seemed to dream.

And he whispered one final phrase to the quiet sky,

I do not need stars to guide me.

Only the silence they leave behind.

He stood.

The ground did not shift.

The wind did not stir.

But something within him had bent.

Not broken. Not mended.

Bent. As the fig tree bends to dusk. As the river bends to stone. As longing bends to breath.

He walked from the rise without ceremony, carrying no bark, no stone, no word, only the ache, and the silence the star left behind.

And that silence remained.

Not empty.

Not unanswered.

Not with words, but with the hush of galaxies breathing in the dark.

Chapter Twenty-five - He Who Carries the Breath

He did not know whether the path he walked had ever been walked before. The stones gave no record. They did not remember footsteps, only weight. The wind did not speak of past travelers. It moved without nostalgia.

He was twenty eight seasons old, though age no longer held form. It rested like dust at the edge of him, felt only when light shifted and the body cast a shadow he did not ask for.

The morning was pale. Not weak, but inward. It did not rise with fire, but with hush. It unspooled gently across the horizon like a scroll left unopened for centuries. And within it, the land breathed.

He had not spoken in days.

The tongue had grown quiet, not from weariness, but from reverence. Words had begun to feel like stone carvings, visible, but rarely alive.

Instead, he listened.

Not to voices, but to silence that carried the ache of stars.

His steps led to a clearing where the trees did not stand, but bent, leaning inward as if whispering to a center that held no flame. The soil was dark, not from fire, but from history. He pressed his heel into it softly, feeling the give of roots beneath the surface.

A sound emerged.

Not from his body.

From the breath below the earth.

It did not speak.

It remembered.

And in that memory, he recalled a dream once left unfinished, light falling through a cracked vessel, the voice of one who said, "Do not chase the light. Become its silence."

There had been a scroll. In the dream, it hovered without hands, its pages unreadable and yet known. Upon it, the phrase curled and shimmered like wind against flame,

> The world is a shadow of your thought.

> Change the thought, and the world reshapes.

> Forget the source, and the shadow returns.

He did not wake with fear from that dream. He woke with ache.

Now the trees around him rustled, not from wind, but from witnessing. He sat among their bowed trunks, the light glimmering above like softened stars, not distant, just quiet.

He placed his hand upon a stone, and it warmed beneath him. Not with heat. With presence.

O source beyond naming,

You who speak through absence,

You who breathe without lung,

I have not sought You to be found.

Only to learn how to remain when You are not.

The stone shimmered for a moment. The shimmer was not light. It was surrender.

And he remembered a story once told in a hush,

A child asked the sky where it kept the names of stars.

The sky did not answer.

The child did not ask again.

But walked beneath every star as if named.

He touched his ribs, felt the shape of breath, not as function, but as echo. Breath carried thought. Thought shaped longing. Longing bore silence.

And silence, he knew, was the first language.

He remained there until the trees whispered no more.

The clearing held its hush as a chapel holds the last syllable of prayer.

Then he stood.

The soil gave gently.

The wind bowed once.

And he walked from the grove, deeper into the ache that sings.

He descended into the valley where the lake waited.

It did not shine.

It breathed.

Its surface lay like tempered silver, unmoving yet alive. Not mirrored, but absorbing. Not distant, but intimate. It held the sky without boasting, the hills without definition. To look upon it was not to see, but to feel.

He approached the water with reverence. Not as pilgrim. Not as wanderer. But as listener.

A cluster of reeds bent low nearby, murmuring in tones too ancient for language. Beneath their roots, fragments stirred, thin shards that glimmered not with gold, but with intention.

He knelt.

The soil there was moist, dark with remembrance. It gave gently beneath his fingers as he uncovered them, scrolls, worn and incomplete, curled like slumbering creatures. Their edges were softened by years beneath the breath of water. Their text faded. Their ink, barely visible.

He did not unroll them. He did not disturb their shape.

Instead, he placed a hand above them, letting his breath fall toward their silence.

And within that hush, verses began to stir, not read, but known.

> I am the one whom they call silence,
>
> I am the memory that does not flee.
>
> I dwell in the marrow of stars.
>
> I whisper, and creation returns to listening.

He touched the nearest fragment, felt its pulse, not literal, but aching.

It spoke of a child born with no name, whose laughter awakened stones.

Of a flame that learned not to burn but to warm.

Of a veil drawn not over eyes, but between questions.

He did not question.

He received.

And within that receiving, the lake shimmered slightly, not in ripples, but in recognition. The wind stilled. The sky dimmed.

He traced a circle in the sand beside him.

Then another.

Then a third.

Not as symbol, not as map, but as breath turned shape.

Beside the scrolls, he placed a stone from his satchel, small, smooth, dark as night's center. It pulsed faintly in his palm before touching earth.

And he whispered,

> Let what was forgotten remain unknown.
>
> Let what was unseen remain unspoken.
>
> But let what was felt return,
>
> not in words,
>
> but in wonder.

A figure passed behind him, without form, without voice. It lingered as presence. Not guiding. Not guarding. Simply there.

He did not turn.

He closed his eyes.

The scrolls trembled once more, then stilled.

And in their stillness, he felt the ache of truths too wide for page.

He stood slowly, leaving the circle unmarred.

The lake did not call. It did not grieve. It continued its breath.

And he walked again, not from scrolls, not from silence, but into the next fold of memory.

Into dusk.

Where wind begins to listen.

He did not return to the cave as one who sought shelter.

He returned as one who knew the rhythm of the stone and the silence behind it.

The entrance was unchanged. Smooth edges, wind-worn, trembling faintly under the hush of night. Within, the shadows had not shifted. They held their contours like a memory too sacred to be rewritten.

He stepped inside and let the dim gather around him. The ceiling curved like an open palm. The floor was cold with stillness. It held no scent of smoke, no echo of footsteps. Only the shape of waiting.

In the far corner, where moonlight pierced through a narrow crevice, he found the stone he remembered, the one where he had once traced spirals without reason, where breath had once become question.

He sat again.

Not as before.

He sat with the presence of the scrolls in his chest, with the voice of the lake in his blood.

He placed the small dark stone on the floor beside him. It hummed faintly.

And then, he closed his eyes.

A figure formed, not of flesh, not of flame, but of curve. It bent like a question left in the mouth of a child. It hovered with the scent of figs and forgotten wind.

It spoke,

I am the first memory.

I am the whisper behind every flame.

I do not teach. I remember.

You do not follow Me. You become Me.

He did not reply.

He listened.

The figure did not remain. It folded inward, becoming not less, but more.

He opened his eyes.

Before him, the stone pulsed once, then stilled.

He placed his palm against it.

And whispered,

Let me not speak to be known.

Let me breathe to remain.

Let me vanish into hush,

not as absence,

but as presence undesiring form.

The wind stirred beyond the cave mouth.

It did not enter.

It watched.

And the night deepened.

Not into fear.

But into fullness.

He remained within the cave until the wind began its descent. It came not as invitation, nor as warning, but as closing refrain, soft as footsteps in dream, steady as dusk's arrival.

Outside, the valley exhaled. The trees resumed their gentle bending, the earth its tender hum. No fire marked the hilltop. No vision pierced the sky. The stone beside him remained warm, quiet, a presence without demand.

He stood slowly, eyes tracing the outline of nothing. Not absence. Not vision. Just stillness shaped into landscape.

And then he stepped forward, one breath at a time.

Not to leave.

But to carry.

The cave did not mourn his parting. It held its shape, its hush, its unlit cradle of questions.

And as he walked from its mouth, the sky did not blaze.

The stars did not whisper.

But the silence they left behind felt more complete than any answer.

Chapter Twenty-six - Breath Before the Whispers

At twenty nine, he had not yet been sent, but the mountains already trembled. Silence, once still, began to speak in breaths of hidden light. The measure of his days was not counted in hours, but in the quiet forging of purpose. Twenty palms of time held nine secrets; each tested in the furnace of the heart. Prophecy was not declared - it was written in absence, prepared in the hush before the call, a call that could not be refused.

No one spoke, but the wind began to lean.

There was breath before word, and word before name.

The wilderness did not stir, but it waited.

In a hush older than stars, He stood, not as a prophet, nor as a boy, but as breath becoming voice.

And the whispers drew near. And the silence did not break, it bloomed. Each shadow in the canyon listened for the syllable not yet born.

He did not step forward.

He unfolded.

Behind him, the stones remembered rivers.

Above him, the sky folded its wings.

Within him, time trembled, as if aware that something unwritten was about to speak.

He stood before the fig tree without fruit.

It did not disappoint.

It waited.

And he understood, not in words, but in pulse, that this morning was not like others. Not for its light, which fell softly. Not for the wind, which moved without asking. But because the ache in the earth had shifted.

The sky was not silent.

It listened.

He knelt, pressing his fingers into soil still damp with night's breath. Beneath the roots, something stirred, not worm, not stone, not scripture.

Memory.

And it spoke, not in voice, but in knowing,

The kingdom is not coming.

It is here, behind your eye, beneath your rib.

It waits for the breath that believes it was always.

The wind circled him, tugging the hem of his robe. A bird flew overhead without call. And he remembered something not taught, not learned, but revealed:

That the light within all things is not broken. It is hidden.

That awakening does not begin with fire.

It begins with stillness that dares to name itself.

He rose, not with haste, but with gravity. His shadow did not follow; it walked ahead, as if the day could not wait.

In the distance, a river turned.

And beyond the turn, a figure stood whose voice would crack heaven, though he would not speak his name.

He moved forward, not as a pilgrim but as one summoned. The figure ahead remained unnamed, not out of mystery, but out of necessity. Some presences defy categorization.

The terrain offered no resistance, but it watched. Every stone, every leaf bore quiet witness. The silence wasn't absence; it was anticipation.

As he approached, the temperature shifted, not colder, not warmer, just aware. Like the air was adjusting to him.

The man didn't speak. There were no words that fit. Language felt inadequate, almost vulgar, in the face of what stood before him.

The figure didn't instruct or gesture. It simply existed, like a threshold in human form. Crossing it wouldn't feel like stepping into another place, but like becoming a different person.

Behind him was time. Ahead, something outside it.

He moved again, slowly. The soles of his feet, worn with the dust of twenty nine seasons under the sun, pressed into the earth with intention. The ground didn't resist; it yielded in quiet recognition. The light ahead remained steady, as if holding its breath.

The figure turned, not fully, merely enough to mark presence. That gesture, almost imperceptible, shifted the air. What had been approach became arrival.

No words passed between them. There was nothing to declare. No need for names or affirmation. The one who stood before him offered nothing in gesture, nothing in speech. He simply was. Not a guardian. Not a mirror. But a weightless presence.

Around them, the terrain held its stillness. Not silence, but attention. The birds remained tucked in absence. The wind had curled away. Even the river past the bend hushed its own pulse, as if listening for truth deeper than sound.

He did not speak. His breath, earned through the long turning of sabbatical moons, already carried the answer. He was not arriving at something new; he was returning to what had long awaited.

The figure stepped back, not departing, but creating space. A gesture of release, not invitation.

He stepped forward. Not toward destiny or rite, but into ground that had known his shaping before memory had formed. The air shifted. The path welcomed him.

No heralds. No titles. Yet everything recognized him.

The air shifted once more, less like wind and more like recognition. It wasn't empty, yet no sound remained. Even breath felt altered, slower, deeper, like it now belonged to something larger.

The ground absorbed his weight differently. There was no resistance. Just accommodation. Dry leaves didn't crack. Stones didn't echo. Every part of the landscape had softened, as if expecting him.

Above, the light changed, not brighter, not dimmer, but thinner. Sunlight passed through branches and dust like it didn't want to intrude. Shadows stretched but held their shape. Nothing moved abruptly.

There were no animal sounds. Not even the distant scrape of wings. Yet the absence wasn't unsettling. It was deliberate. Birds had paused. Insects had quieted. The canyon held still. Even the river bent around its own noise.

He glanced at his hands. They looked the same, but the space around them felt charged, like the moment before rain, before a blade meets stone, before speech chooses form. Everything waited, but not passively. The hush wasn't silence. It was focus.

Then the horizon leaned inward. Not visually, but viscerally. The edges of space, dust, branch, sky, stone, came closer, not to press, but to surround. The hush became physical.

This was not calm. It was contact.

And he remained still, not out of reverence, but necessity. Movement would interrupt something sacred. For now, everything that needed to happen was already happening.

The hush thickened. It wasn't quiet anymore, it was presence. A pressure without weight. A density without form. The world hadn't stopped. It had steadied.

Everything waited, not for permission, but for alignment.

He stood still, no longer measuring time in motion, but in resonance. The breath in his chest felt older than his body. It wasn't rhythm. It was arrival.

There were no landmarks here. The river no longer turned, it paused. The canyon walls didn't echo; they retained. Even the air had ceased shifting. Its silence had texture, and it folded around him with intention.

From the edges of the landscape, light retreated, not to hide, but to let shadow sharpen. He was not surrounded, he was centered. Not placed in the middle of something but pressed to its meaning.

The figure ahead remained unchanged. No gesture, no movement. But something passed between them. Not speech. Not glance. Just knowing. It carried more weight than language could bear.

Behind him, the long stretch of seasons braided themselves into memory. The soles of his feet, callused from sacred distances, settled. Not as wanderer. Not as messenger. But as presence in equilibrium.

The breath before the whispers was full. It held every silence he'd ever entered. Every unanswered question. Every ache beneath the ribcage.

And in that moment, the world didn't ask anything of him. It simply waited for him to remember what it had always known.

He took another step forward.

There was no response.

But the ground felt different underfoot, cooler, more precise. As though it had been waiting for that single moment to begin existing.

He didn't look back. Not because he refused to, but because there was nothing left to return to. The past was folded now, quiet, complete, watching from its place in the dust.

Ahead was not promise.

It was presence.

He did not move for a moment that eclipsed time, not in absence, but in reverence. Each inhale did not take air, it gave recognition. The hush had stopped listening. Now, it began to remember.

All around him, the terrain shimmered, not visibly, but perceptibly. It had absorbed every waiting. The silence had thickened into fabric, stitched with threads not seen, but felt. Beneath his feet, the earth no longer yielded. It supported with intent. Not ground, it was response.

Above, the light shifted again, as though tomorrow had begun rehearsing. It came not in brilliance, but in subtlety, the color of breath held in morning's throat.

He raised his eyes, not for vision, but for awareness. And the figure ahead, still unmoved, began to dissolve, not like mist, nor ghost, but like language after truth.

In its place, not emptiness.

Presence.

He understood then, this was not meeting. It was merging. Not communion of persons, but of pulse. This was the thinning veil, where what is known remembers being unnamed.

Every particle around him held its place with clarity, as if the cosmos itself had exhaled to make room.

He did not ask questions.

He had become their answer.

His hands, once witnesses of labor and longing, now glowed, not with light, but with memory refracted. Time itself, having waited, now leaned gently toward him, like an elder ready to hand over its final story.

He stood not as emissary, nor messiah.

He stood as opening.

One step more. Not toward destination, but toward echo. The ground met him midstride, no resistance, only welcome. The canyon behind him exhaled, the stones settled, and the river began its turning once again.

The birds did not resume. The wind did not return. But something deeper began to hum, beneath the soil, behind the sky, within the breath of things. It wasn't sound.

It was readiness.

Ahead lay no throne, no scroll, no altar. But the path shimmered with the ache of arrival. It would not carry him.

It would recognize him.

The final hush wrapped itself around his shoulders, not as mantle, not as mission, but as acknowledgment. The robe moved with its own rhythm now, caught in the slow dance of becoming.

He breathed once more, and this time the air responded with form. He was no longer moving through the world.

He was becoming its word.

Tomorrow waited, not in distance, but in unveiling. Its cusp was not a boundary, it was an inhale before the name, a blink before the story, a silence so full it could only bloom into voice.

And he stepped into it.

Not as what he had been.

But as what had always waited.

Chapter Twenty-seven - Whispered By Stars

He walked into morning without destination. The hills did not greet him, they aligned. The dust no longer clung, it parted. And above him, stars invisible in daylight still whispered, not in constellation, but in intent.

They had whispered him into being, long before time had a calendar. Not by name, but by presence. Not as arrival, but as necessity.

The valley opened wide as if exhaling, not to guide but to yield. The trees drew no attention, but they shifted subtly, a branch lowering, a leaf turning, as though the forest had learned him long ago.

Somewhere ahead, a figure waited, not out of patience, but because waiting was the only form reverence could take. The road was not empty. It was expectant.

He passed stone and stream, neither murmuring nor still. They witnessed him as one might witness weather reshaping a mountain, slow, inevitable, intimate.

The final breath before word had begun. Not spoken, not forged, simply rising.

And in the pause between pulses, the land remembered a promise etched into dust before law, spoken in silence before voice. He did not step into revelation.

He was revelation unfolding.

The wind had not returned, yet its absence had texture. The trees did not speak, yet their branches leaned. Each step forward was a sentence remembered by the soil, a line of truth written not in ink but in weight.

He had passed the final turning of age, the thirtieth orbit marked, not by ceremony, but by how the sky seemed to hold him differently. Not with gravity, but with recognition. He was no longer walking into years. He was walking out of them.

The path narrowed, not physically, but in meaning. Surroundings sharpened. Dust lifted before contact. Even shadows, those quiet keepers of form, began folding toward him. It was not reverence. It was response.

A stone, long buried beneath vine and root, revealed itself. Not through movement, but by emergence. As if it had waited beneath centuries of silence for this exact moment. He stepped past it, and it settled. Not as obstacle, but as witness.

The air grew dense. Not humid, not heavy. Just aware.

Even time, long steady in its stretch, began to bend. Moments didn't pass; they hovered. Light didn't fall; it listened. The terrain wasn't guiding him. It was opening.

Stars, buried behind the daylight, pressed closer. Not visibly. But their pressure pulsed beneath skin and sky, whispering not direction, but memory. They weren't shining, they were remembering him.

Ahead, the land unfolded. Hills grew quiet. Trees ceased motion. A single line of stone cut across the horizon, not a wall, not a ridge, but the edge of what had been waiting.

And then, without signal, without sign, the soundless unfolding reached its breath.

The birds returned.

But they did not cry out. They moved in formation, quiet arcs across the morning. Their wings cut space in deliberate sequence, writing without language what the earth could not say aloud.

In that moment, everything shifted, not into climax, but into coordination. All things now leaned forward, not to point, but to reveal.

The hush broke, not in noise, but in readiness.

And the path did not ascend.

It extended.

He did not falter.

He stepped forward.

Not into legacy.

But into the space where history holds its breath.

It was not a path in the ordinary sense, no discernible trail, no footsteps carved into soil. The land simply opened. Dunes shifted with deliberation, stones reassembled into memory, and the wind, though subtle, began to behave like a script being rehearsed. It was as if the earth itself had agreed not to lead, but to allow.

He stepped into this stretch of terrain, not with certainty but with a stillness born of listening. the unspoken ritual of solitude, and now, movement. The wilderness did not greet him, nor resist him. It merely endured, as if waiting had become its native tongue.

He walked with the poise of someone both lost and ordained. Every plant, brittlebush, acacia, the cracked tumble of root systems, seemed to pull inward, hushed not by fear, but by reverence. A fig tree stood half flowering, bearing fruit on one limb and silence on the other. He did not pick. He noted. He continued.

Above him, the sky bent into gradients not seen by his peers. The blue was more cobalt than serene, touched with a pallor of stars that refused to sleep, even by daylight. Each cloud rehearsed its role in some silent liturgy, moving in positions like priests veiled in incense. Something ancient moved among them, timeless, yes, but also tender, cautious not to awaken too quickly.

And beneath his feet, the soil whispered. Not with words, but with granular impressions, the sediment of wandering, the softened skeletons of migrations long gone. He felt them, the past steps of prophets, of those unnamed and forgotten, folded into the geology like psalms too sacred to be spoken aloud.

Ahead, the terrain did not rise or fall. It breathed. It allowed. There would be no revelation here, not yet. Only quiet recognition that he had entered something older than maps and deeper than stories. The wilderness was not a test. It was a mirror.

The sky did not brighten, yet something behind it began to wake. Not in color, but in pressure. What had once been void now felt dense, as though the stars, hidden from the eye, leaned closer, not in orbit, but in awareness.

They had tracked him since the uncounted beginnings, long before the thirtieth turning shaped the weight of his stride. Their glow, though absent by day, stirred within the dust, light remembered by stone, warmth folded into shadow. The constellations were not maps. They were memories. They carried no message, only recognition.

He did not look up. He did not need to. The stars had already settled into the rhythm of his pulse.

Each step forward caused a ripple, not in space, but in meaning. The distance between atoms grew reverent. Particles paused, waiting to realign. Even light behaved differently. It didn't illuminate. It translated.

Somewhere in the vast, unreachable vault, a single star pulsed out of sequence, not violently, but with a hum that softened the edges of gravity. Others followed, their brilliance folding inward, not to dim, but to listen.

He stepped past a pool of still water. It did not reflect his form. It showed orbit.

He reached a clearing where the air thinned and thickened in the same breath. Here, there was no wind. No sound. Only curvature, space bending gently inward, as if embracing without touch.

And in that stillness, above bark and bone, the stars whispered.

They whispered not to guide, but to mark. Not to foretell, but to remember.

They had whispered to him once; when the sky was young and breath was unshaped. And now, they whispered again, not of future, but of readiness.

One star broke silence entirely. Not in brilliance, but in depth. It dimmed to shadow, as if giving its light to the ground below.

The clearing held that light.

He walked through it.

Not into prophecy.

But into the echo of something the stars had never stopped saying.

He paused at the mouth of a ravine, where the air gathered not in gusts, but in decision. Everything had held its breath, not for arrival, but for recognition. The landscape felt suspended. Its silence was not absence, but focus.

Breath had followed him since the first morning, when light touched his face before names had meaning. Now, it thickened, not with weight, but with intent. Even his own inhale seemed shared. Not his alone, but part of the rhythm that carried mountain, root, and memory.

The terrain didn't shift. It refined. Dust aligned along his path as if magnetized by purpose. The edges of rock had softened, curving where they had once broken. Light sat still atop each surface, refraining from shimmer, patient, deliberate, unassuming.

Beneath his ribs, something opened. Not pain, not impulse. Just acknowledgment. The breath he carried had never been singular. It was folded from generations, pressed into his chest by time's quiet hand.

He stepped forward.

A moment later, the earth registered it, not with tremor, but with a hum that seemed to rise from under centuries. It traveled no distance. It arrived everywhere at once.

The sky shifted shade. Not darker. Just deeper.

His next breath did not feed him. It named him. Not with word, but with resonance. A naming without syllable. A recognition without introduction.

In that breath, the ache of creation stirred. Hills leaned inward, not collapsing, but bearing witness. The horizon stretched, not wide, but ancient, flexing as if memory had physical shape.

Silence rose around him, like mist without moisture. Its texture was origin. Its scent held firelight and fig root, cave shadow and mother's gaze. The things that remembered him before he remembered himself.

The next inhale bent light.

The exhale bent time.

No figure had yet spoken. No water had yet rippled. Yet something elemental had begun to turn. The breath, the true breath, the first and last, now stood at the threshold.

And still, no voice.

Only readiness.

The banks weren't marked. No altar. No monument. Just sediment shaped by time and the quiet insistence of water. It had carved the river slowly, with the patience of a presence that expected no recognition, only arrival.

He approached the edge not to reach, but to be reached. The sky dimmed, not in shadow, but in tone. Clouds thinned overhead, forming pale circles as if sky itself were observing from behind its veil.

A figure stood beyond the bend. Not tall. Not distant. Just placed. Not waiting, but positioned, like an old truth leaning into its own moment. The robes hung loose, moving less by wind and more by something beneath the skin of the world.

They didn't look at one another. Not yet.

The water stirred. A ripple, a pause. Then stillness again. It wasn't disturbed by presence. It received it.

He stepped into the clearing, not as stranger, not as heir, but as one who had fulfilled the geography of breath.

The figure moved, barely. A hand shifted, not toward, not away, but like wind cresting in the throat of a mountain. Then stillness resumed.

The river mirrored nothing. No form. No face. It held only sky and motion. And both figures, unnamed, became part of it.

Birds hovered beyond sight. Their wings didn't flap, they balanced, weightless above trees that did not respond. Even the insects had quieted. The entire clearing behaved like a held note.

He didn't kneel. He didn't speak.

He arrived.

The figure did not acknowledge, not immediately. Only when the stillness became substance, when breath had traced its full circle through limb and light, did the space between them begin to take shape.

And in that moment, nothing declared itself.

But everything knew.

He did not wait for direction. Nothing had pointed. Nothing had named. Yet the way forward felt precise, as if the terrain had rehearsed this walk long before his feet touched it.

The figure by the river remained, steady as myth, unchanged by presence yet somehow fulfilled by it. Still, no words passed between them. Still, no gesture revealed intent. But everything in the air held shape now, not of command, but of convergence.

He stepped again. Not further. Not faster. Simply into place.

And the earth adjusted.

Light behaved differently. It didn't land; it lingered. Dust floated longer before settling. A leaf held midair, caught in pause, then fell so slowly it seemed to trace time backward. Every inch of the path ahead existed not in distance, but in decision.

He wasn't ascending.

He wasn't leaving.

He was becoming.

The mountain didn't rise to greet him. It held form, silent and immense, as though sculpted for this moment alone. Even the river, once still, began to move, not with rush, but with acknowledgment. Its surface reflected nothing. It became mirrorless.

He passed through a fold in the land, where wind no longer blew, it leaned. Where breath didn't cycle, it stayed. In this place, gravity and grace behaved the same.

Beneath his robe, the ache of thirty passages pressed gently against his ribs. Not pain, but pressure. A whisper of readiness. Not the kind that demands, but the kind that has waited.

He turned his head, not toward the figure, but toward the horizon. It held nothing spectacular. No flame. No call. Just the road.

And in the distance, the road did not curve.

It welcomed.

One step.

Then another.

Time did not follow.

It observed.

The birds began to move again, slow arcs over brush and sky. The trees resumed their lean. The dust behind him settled in new shape. Everything changed, but nothing declared it.

He did not know the name of the moment.

But it knew him.

And as he stepped from the hush into the opening, not to depart but to unfold, the figure turned, not fully, not finally, but enough.

Enough to let the road begin.

The wind paused, not silenced, but held in a posture of listening.

He had walked through stillness so deep that even memory could not echo within it. Around him, space expanded, not horizontally, but through meaning. Mountains did not loom, they observed. Stars did not glitter, they leaned inward. The path no longer led forward. It led through.

And at its threshold, a figure waited.

Not cloaked.

Not radiant.

Simply present.

Older than the ache of exile. Familiar as childhood's scent of olive bark split beneath a morning sun. The kind of presence that had once split seas, shattered tablets, wept in wilderness, called down fire, held silence above chaos, whispered into wombs.

No name came.

None was needed.

And no introductions were made.

Only breath, measured and complete, drawing the space between them thin. The figure was neither tall nor aged. But every atom around him knew it had once bowed.

A voice came, not from mouth, nor mind, but from the ache behind ribs. A sound that came before sound existed.

You carry what was never given. You bear what was never spoken. You walk where only echo dared go.

The young man did not answer.

He did not need to.

Everything within him leaned toward the truth behind those words. He had not sought them. He had not earned them. Yet they belonged to him as light belongs to flame.

The figure stepped forward, not with movement, but with unfolding.

And the mountains shifted in their stance.

The dust stilled midair.

The birds circled wider.

The wind slowed, listening.

"The silence that called you was not empty, it was full. You did not come here to be known. You came here to remember."

Every step that had carried him, every hour beneath the sun, every moment of ache, solitude, clarity, hunger, had led to this.

Not to arrival.

But to unveiling.

Those who once spoke fire into stone, who danced with chariots in whirlwinds, who knew the name that could not be spoken; they are here. Not to declare. To witness.

And suddenly, more figures formed.

Not summoned.

But remembered.

Their outlines made not of form, but of consequence. They stood in positions worn through centuries of prayer. Each carried silence as language.

One stepped forward, robe pressed with dust of seventy generations, eyes bearing the sorrow of nations torn too early from truth.

Another knelt, not in submission, but in weight, arms inscribed with stories carved before scroll, before quill, before breath.

A third raised their gaze, not toward him, but toward what was becoming through him.

They said nothing.

Their presence said everything.

And then, the figure who had first appeared extended his hand.

Not as offering.

Not as command.

But as invitation.

"The river behind you knows your weight. The path ahead will not recognize your name. You are no longer waiting for permission. You are the permission."

Light narrowed around them, forming not halo, but horizon. It bent, not to glorify, but to align. And in that bending, time itself found posture.

"Go."

Not shouted.

Not whispered.

But stated in a way that breathes inside stone.

Not to speak. Not to gather. Not to rule.

The young man's chest rose.

He did not nod.

He did not bow.

He walked.

Through the circle of presence.

Through the moment that unraveled heaven's veil.

Through what had always waited, not for him, but within him.

The wind pressed behind.

The river stilled beside.

The figures did not follow.

But they remained.

Witnesses not to action, but to alignment.

And as he walked, sky widened.

The light grew neither brighter nor dimmer, but truer.

And one final breath, drawn by the figure behind him, pushed the moment into permanence,

"Go, to become what cannot be forgotten."

He stepped forward, not into wilderness.

But into the threshold of what wilderness dreams of becoming.

And all the world did not bow.

It adjusted.

The birds ceased their circles.

The trees shifted their roots.

Even the silence grew louder, as if preparing to house new meaning.

The figures behind him blurred, not into mist, but into memory.

And the truth echoed, not in words, but in consequence.

No crown waited.

No crowd assembled.

Only the soil, holding breath.

Only the light stretching forward.

Only the ache in the ribs of the world, where prophecy had waited long enough.

He had not come to fulfill.

He had come to begin.

Bernd L. Bergmann is an author, senior technology educator, and caregiver based in Montana. He teaches older adults how to navigate modern devices with confidence and clarity, works as a driver and soon to be CNA at a health care and rehabilitation center. His writing blends poetic reflection with spiritual curiosity, exploring the quiet places where memory, mystery, and the sacred meet. Midrash Whispered by Stars is his first published book, part of a growing body of contemplative work shaped by lived experience, compassion, and a lifelong fascination with the stories that continue to whisper beneath the surface of tradition.

www.ingramcontent.com/pod-product-compliance
Lightning Source LLC
LaVergne TN
LVHW041315080426

835513LV00008B/462